PORTO TRAVEL
GUIDE 2025

Carlos Costa Martin

*Copyright © **Carlos Costa Martin** 2025. All rights reserved. No part of this publication may be reproduced, distributed, or transmitted in any form or by any means, including photocopying, recording, or other electronic or mechanical methods, without the prior written permission of the publisher, except in the case of brief quotations embodied in critical reviews and certain other noncommercial uses permitted by copyright law.*

Table of Contents

Introduction... 10
   Welcome To Porto.. 10
   Brief History of Porto... 15
   Suggested Itinerary.. 20
   Best Time to visit... 25
Getting There and around..**28**
   Getting Around Porto.. 30
Neighborhoods..**36**
   Ribeira... 36
   Miragaia.. 42
   Cedofeita... 46
   Boavista.. 49
   Foz... 55
   Gaia... 57
Culture...**60**
   Traditions.. 60
   Language... 63
   Festivals.. 66
   Monuments... 71
   Museums.. 75

Outdoor **79**
    Cruises 79
    Gardens 81
    Beaches 83
    Hiking 86
    Cycling 89
Food **92**
    Dishes 92
    Restaurants 94
    Cafés 97
    Wine 100
    Markets 103
Where to Stay **105**
    Hotels 105
    Hostels 108
    Boutique 110
    Airbnb 112
Nightlife **114**
    Bars 114
    Fado 117
    Rooftops 120
    Music 122
Education **125**
    Schools 125
    Universities 130

Tips... 132
    Safety.. 133
    Etiquette... 134
    Money.. 137
    Phrases... 140
Conclusion...143

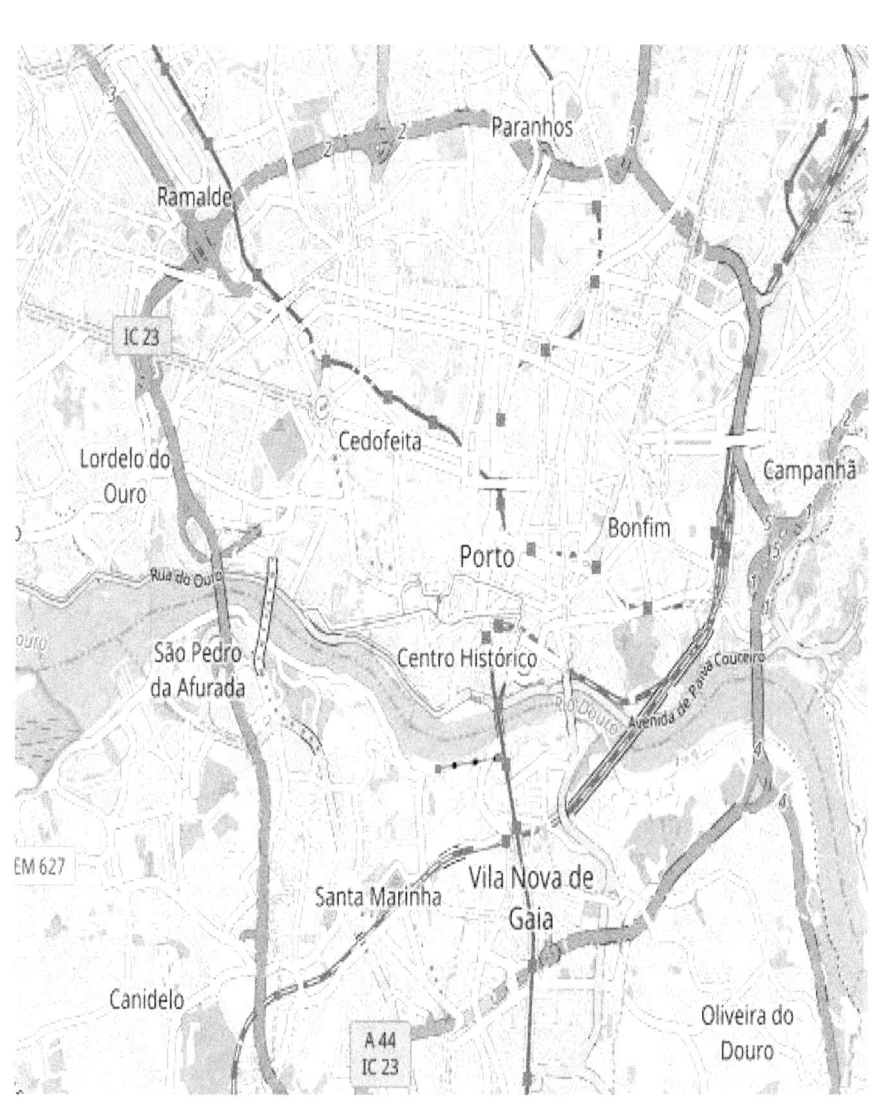

Porto, Portugal | OpenStreetMap

Largo da Pena Ventosa in Porto, Portugal. Quiet square in old city centre

Porto, Porto District, Portugal

Scenic View of Porto's Dom Luís I Bridge and Douro River

Introduction

Welcome To Porto

I arrived in Porto with a light bag and an open mind, expecting to see the usual sights that any traveler might tick off a list. But what I experienced in those few days was far more than just a visual appreciation of the city—it was an immersion into a place that seemed to exist in multiple timelines at once.

The first morning, I walked from my accommodation near Trindade Station toward the river. The streets were already alive with activity, though not in a rushed or chaotic way. It was the kind of movement that comes from a city at ease with itself. Elderly men stood outside cafés, stirring sugar into their espressos with slow, deliberate movements. Shopkeepers arranged fresh pastries in their windows, the scent of butter and cinnamon spilling onto the pavement.

I had no rigid plans, only a vague idea of where I wanted to go. My first stop was the São Bento train station, a place I had read about but wasn't prepared for in reality. The tiled walls told stories of Portugal's past, from royal processions to agricultural life. I found myself lost in the details, scanning each blue-and-white panel as if they were pages in a book. Commuters passed by, seemingly indifferent to the grandeur surrounding them, but for me, it was like stepping into a piece of history frozen in time.

From São Bento, I made my way down toward the Ribeira district. The descent toward the river was lined with narrow streets, some so steep that I had to pause and brace myself before continuing. The buildings, with their wrought-iron balconies and laundry hanging out to dry, felt both old and lived-in. It was clear that Porto had not been polished for tourists—it had remained authentic, carrying its scars with quiet pride.

When I reached the banks of the Douro River, the first thing that struck me was the light. The sun reflected off the water in a way that made the entire city look like a painting. Boats, some modern and others resembling old trade vessels, bobbed along the surface. Across the river, Vila Nova de Gaia stood with its rows of port wine cellars, the names of famous brands painted in bold letters on the rooftops.

I took a seat at an outdoor café and ordered a glass of vinho verde. The server, noticing my curiosity about the wine, explained that it was young and slightly effervescent, perfect for a warm afternoon. As I sipped, I watched a group of street musicians setting up nearby. They played a mix of traditional Portuguese songs and reworked versions of familiar tunes, drawing in a small crowd.

Feeling restless after a while, I decided to cross the Dom Luís I Bridge on foot. The structure, designed by a student of Gustave Eiffel, was both intimidating and impressive. As I walked along the upper deck, with trams occasionally rattling past, I caught sight of people standing on the railings. It took me a moment to realize what they were doing—diving into the river below. A mix of locals and daredevil tourists were taking turns leaping off the bridge, disappearing into the deep blue water before surfacing to the sound of cheers.

Once on the Gaia side, I followed the signs leading to one of the smaller port wine cellars. Unlike the large commercial tours, this one felt more intimate. The guide explained the process of making port, from the handpicked grapes in the Douro Valley to the aging process in oak barrels. The tasting session was a revelation. I had expected port to be overly sweet and heavy, but the variations—from dry white to rich, aged tawny—were complex and layered. Each sip carried the weight of centuries of tradition.

By early evening, I was back in Porto, wandering through the streets near Clérigos Tower. The sun was beginning to set, casting long shadows on the buildings. I stumbled upon Livraria Lello, a bookstore famous for its connection to J.K. Rowling. While the line outside was long, I decided to wait. Once inside, the carved wooden staircase and stained-glass ceiling made it clear why this place was so revered. Even if I hadn't known about its literary significance, the sheer craftsmanship of the space was enough to make it special.

Hunger led me toward a small family-run restaurant, one of those places where the menu is handwritten and only in Portuguese. I ordered francesinha, a sandwich layered with cured meats, covered in melted cheese, and drenched in a thick, beer-based sauce. It was served with a side of crispy fries, and from the first bite, I understood why it was a local favorite. It wasn't just food—it was a meal designed for comfort, the kind that made you want to linger at the table long after finishing.

Later that night, I found myself back along the river, this time on a terrace with a view of the cityscape illuminated against the dark sky. A few tables away, a group of people broke into spontaneous fado singing, their voices carrying a kind of melancholic beauty that felt deeply tied to Porto itself.

As I walked back to my accommodation, I realized what had made this trip so memorable. It wasn't just the sights or the food—it was the way the city moved at its own rhythm, welcoming but never demanding. Porto didn't ask to be admired; it simply existed, offering its stories to those willing to notice.

Brief History of Porto

Early Settlement and Roman Era

Porto's origins date back to pre-Roman times, when Celtic and Iberian tribes settled in the region. By the 4th century BC, a small community existed along the Douro River. When the Romans arrived in the 1st century BC, they recognized Porto's strategic location for trade and military purposes. They built roads and fortified the area, calling it Portus Cale, which is believed to be the origin of the name Portugal. Under Roman rule, Porto became a key port for the export of agricultural goods, metals, and ceramics.

Germanic and Moorish Invasions (5th-11th Century)

After the fall of the Roman Empire, Porto went through periods of instability. In the 5th century, the Suebi, a Germanic tribe, took control of the region, making Braga their capital. By the early 8th century, the Moors arrived in the Iberian Peninsula, conquering large parts of Portugal, including Porto. However, their rule in the north was short-lived. The Christian Reconquista, which aimed to reclaim land from Muslim rule, saw Porto being retaken by Christian forces in the 9th century.

The Formation of Portugal and Porto's Role (12th-15th Century)

Porto played a significant role in the foundation of Portugal as an independent kingdom. In 1096, Count Henry of Burgundy was granted the County of Portugal, which included Porto. His son, Afonso Henriques, later declared independence from the Kingdom of León and was recognized as Portugal's first king in 1143. Porto became a vital trading hub, exporting wine, olive oil, and textiles. By the 14th century, it had established strong trade connections with England, a relationship that led to the famous Treaty of Windsor in 1386, one of the oldest alliances in history.

The Age of Exploration (15th-16th Century)

During Portugal's Age of Exploration, Porto contributed to the expansion of maritime trade. Henry the Navigator, a key figure in Portugal's exploration efforts, had connections to the city. Porto shipbuilders supplied vessels that were used in the voyages to Africa, India, and the Americas. Unlike Lisbon, which became the center of colonial administration, Porto remained focused on commerce, particularly in the wine trade.

The Growth of the Port Wine Industry (17th-18th Century)

By the 17th century, Porto became synonymous with port wine. The English demand for Portuguese wine increased after England imposed heavy taxes on French imports. In 1703, the Methuen Treaty strengthened trade ties between England and Portugal, giving preferential treatment to Portuguese wines. The Douro Valley became the primary wine-producing region, with Porto serving as the main export hub. To regulate the quality of wine production, the Marquis of Pombal established the world's first wine demarcation system in 1756.

The Napoleonic Invasions and Civil War (19th Century)

The 19th century was turbulent for Porto. In 1807, Napoleon's army invaded Portugal, leading to a period of resistance. The city suffered from looting and destruction before being liberated by British and Portuguese forces. Later, Porto became a center of political conflict during the Liberal Wars (1828-1834) between absolutists and constitutionalists. In 1832, the Siege of Porto saw supporters of liberalism, led by King Pedro IV, resisting a blockade for over a year. The victory of the liberals shaped Portugal's transition toward a constitutional monarchy.

Industrialization and Urban Expansion (Late 19th-20th Century)

Porto industrialized rapidly in the late 19th century. Factories, railways, and bridges were built, modernizing the city's economy. The construction of the Dom Luís I Bridge in 1886, designed by a student of Gustave Eiffel, symbolized Porto's modernization. During the 20th century, the city continued to expand, with neighborhoods developing beyond the historic center. However, political instability, including the dictatorship of António Salazar (1932-1974), slowed progress. Porto played a role in the Carnation Revolution of 1974, which ended Salazar's authoritarian regime and restored democracy.

Porto in the Modern Era (21st Century)

Since the early 2000s, Porto has undergone extensive revitalization. The city was designated as a UNESCO World Heritage Site in 1996, recognizing its architectural and historical significance. Tourism grew rapidly, driven by its cultural heritage, port wine cellars, and vibrant atmosphere. The opening of the Porto Metro in 2002 improved transportation, and in 2012, Porto was named Europe's Best Destination. Today, Porto balances its rich history with modern innovation, attracting visitors from around the world.

Porto's history reflects resilience, trade, and cultural significance, making it one of the most historically important cities in Portugal.

Suggested Itinerary

Planning a week in Porto offers a rich blend of history, culture, and gastronomy. Below is a detailed seven-day itinerary to help you experience the best of this vibrant city and its surroundings.

Day 1: Exploring Porto's Historic Center

Morning: São Bento Station and Porto Cathedral (Sé do Porto)

São Bento Station*: Begin at this historic train station renowned for its azulejo tile panels depicting Portugal's history.*

Address*: Praça de Almeida Garrett, 4000-069 Porto*

Opening Hours*: Daily, 5:00 AM – 12:00 AM*

Admission*: Free*
Porto Cathedral*: A short walk away, this 12th-century cathedral offers panoramic city views.*
Address*: Terreiro da Sé, 4050-573 Porto*

Opening Hours*: Daily, 9:00 AM – 6:30 PM*

Admission*: Free; Cloister access: €3*

Afternoon: Ribeira District

Stroll through the UNESCO-listed Ribeira neighborhood, characterized by narrow streets and colorful houses.

Enjoy lunch at a riverside café, sampling local dishes like **francesinha** or grilled sardines.

Evening: Douro River Cruise

Take a traditional **rabelo** boat cruise to view Porto's six bridges.

Departure Point: Cais da Ribeira

Duration: Approximately 50 minutes

Cost: Around €15 per person

Day 2: Art, Literature, and Panoramic Views

Morning: Livraria Lello and Clérigos Tower

Livraria Lello: Visit one of the world's most beautiful bookstores, known for its neo-Gothic architecture.

Address: Rua das Carmelitas 144, 4050-161 Porto

Opening Hours: Daily, 9:30 AM – 7:00 PM

Admission: €5, deductible from book purchases

Clérigos Tower: Climb 225 steps for a panoramic city view.

Address: Rua de São Filipe de Nery, 4050-546 Porto

Opening Hours: Daily, 9:00 AM – 7:00 PM

Admission: €6

Afternoon: Bolhão Market and Rua de Santa Catarina

Bolhão Market: Explore this traditional market offering fresh produce, meats, and cheeses.

Address: Rua Formosa, 4000-214 Porto

Opening Hours: Monday–Friday, 8:00 AM – 8:00 PM; Saturday, 8:00 AM – 6:00 PM

Rua de Santa Catarina: Porto's main shopping street, featuring boutiques and the historic **Café Majestic**.

Café Majestic Address: Rua de Santa Catarina 112, 4000-442 Porto

Opening Hours: Monday–Saturday, 9:00 AM – 11:30 PM

Evening: Fado Show

Experience traditional Portuguese music at a local **fado** house.

Example Venue: Casa da Mariquinhas

Address: Rua de São Sebastião 25, 4050-569 Porto

Showtimes: Typically around 9:00 PM

Admission: Varies; approximately €15

Day 3: Wine and Coastal Charm

Morning: Port Wine Cellar Tour

Graham's Port Lodge: Tour the cellars and enjoy tastings.

Address: Rua do Agro 141, 4400-281 Vila Nova de Gaia

Opening Hours: Daily, 9:30 AM – 6:00 PM

Tour Cost: Starting at €15

Afternoon: Foz do Douro

Take tram line 1 from Infante to Foz, Porto's coastal district.

Tram Fare: €3 one-way

Walk along **Praia dos Ingleses** and **Praia do Molhe**.

Visit **Fortaleza de São João da Foz**, a 16th-century fortress.

Address: Esplanada do Castelo, 4150-196 Porto

Opening Hours: Varies; typically 10:00 AM – 5:00 PM

Admission: Free

Evening: Seafood Dinner

23

*Dine at **Restaurante Marisqueira Antiga**, known for fresh seafood.*

Address*: Rua Heróis de França 633, 4450-159 Matosinhos*

Opening Hours*: Daily, 12:00 PM – 11:00 PM*

Average Cost*:*

Best Time to visit

Porto, Portugal's second-largest city, offers a variety of experiences throughout the year. The ideal time to visit depends on your preferences regarding weather, crowd sizes, and local events. Here's a breakdown to help you decide:

Spring (March to May)

Spring in Porto brings mild temperatures, averaging between 15°C and 20°C (59°F to 68°F). This season is ideal for outdoor activities and sightseeing without the summer crowds. April and May are particularly pleasant, offering blooming landscapes and comfortable weather.

Key Events:

Fantasporto: An international fantasy film festival held annually in late February to early March, showcasing a range of genre films.

Summer (June to August)

Summer is peak tourist season in Porto, with temperatures ranging from 18°C to 25°C (64°F to 77°F). The city is lively, and many festivals take place during this time. However, popular attractions can be crowded, and accommodation prices may rise.

Key Events:

25

São João Festival*:*
Celebrated on the night of June 23rd, this festival is one of Porto's most significant events, featuring street parties, fireworks, and traditional customs.

NOS Primavera Sound*: A music festival typically held in early June, attracting international and local artists.*

Autumn (September to November)

Autumn offers mild temperatures and fewer tourists, making it a favorable time to visit. September is particularly suitable for wine enthusiasts, as it's the grape harvest season in the nearby Douro Valley.

Key Events:

Porto Wine Fest*: Usually held in September, this festival celebrates the city's rich wine heritage with tastings, workshops, and live music.*

Winter (December to February)

Winters in Porto are mild but wetter, with temperatures averaging around 10°C (50°F). This season sees fewer tourists, leading to lower accommodation prices. While some outdoor activities might be limited due to rain, indoor attractions remain accessible.

Key Events:

Christmas Markets*: Throughout December, Porto hosts festive markets offering local crafts, foods, and*

26

holiday decorations.

New Year's Eve: *The city celebrates with fireworks and concerts, particularly around the Ribeira district.*

The best time to visit Porto depends on your preferences:

Spring (March to May): *Pleasant weather and blooming landscapes.*

Summer (June to August): *Vibrant festivals and warm temperatures but larger crowds.*

Autumn (September to November): *Mild climate, fewer tourists, and wine-related events.*

Winter (December to February): *Cooler, wetter weather with festive celebrations and lower prices.*

Each season offers a unique experience, ensuring a memorable visit to Porto year-round.

Getting There and around

Porto, Portugal

Navigating Porto and its environs is both straightforward and enjoyable, thanks to a comprehensive and efficient transportation network. Here's an in-depth guide to getting to and around Porto, complete with practical details to enhance your journey.

Arriving in Porto

Most travelers reach Porto via the Francisco Sá Carneiro Airport (OPO), situated approximately 11 kilometers northwest of the city center. This modern airport serves numerous international and domestic flights, making it a convenient gateway to the region.

- ***Metro:*** *The Metro do Porto's Line E (Purple Line) provides a direct connection from the airport to the city center. Trains depart every 20 to 30 minutes, depending on the time of day, and the journey to Trindade Station takes about 30 minutes. A single journey ticket costs €2.75. citeturn0search1*

- ***Buses:*** *Several bus lines, including STCP routes 601, 602, and 604, connect the airport to various parts of Porto. Tickets can be purchased onboard for €1.95.*

- ***Taxis and Rideshares:*** *Taxis are readily available at the airport, with fares to the city center averaging around €25. Rideshare services like Uber also operate in Porto, offering competitive rates and the convenience of app-based bookings.*

Getting Around Porto

Once in Porto, a variety of transportation options are at your disposal to explore the city's attractions and neighborhoods.

- ***Metro:*** *Porto's metro system is efficient and covers a broad area, including six lines that reach many key destinations. Trains typically run from 6:00 AM to 1:00 AM, with frequencies varying by line and time of day.*

- ***Buses:*** *The STCP operates an extensive bus network throughout Porto and neighboring municipalities. Buses are a reliable option for reaching areas not served by the metro.*

- ***Trams:*** *For a nostalgic experience, Porto's historic trams are a delightful way to see the city, especially along routes that showcase the riverside and historic districts.*

- ***Andante Card:*** *For unlimited travel on Porto's public transportation, consider the Andante Tour card. The 1-day version costs €7.50, and the 3-day version is €16.*

- ***Walking:*** *Porto's compact city center makes walking a pleasant and practical way to explore its narrow streets, historic sites, and vibrant neighborhoods.*

Public Transportation Tickets and Passes

Porto's public transportation system operates on a zone-based fare system, and the Andante card is the primary ticketing method.

- ***Andante Azul:*** *This non-personalized, rechargeable paper ticket is suitable for occasional travelers. It can be loaded with single journeys or 24-hour passes. The card itself costs €0.60.*

- ***Andante Tour:*** *Designed for tourists, this card offers unlimited travel across the metro, buses, and some regional trains within the selected time frame. The 24-hour card is priced at €7.50, while the 72-hour card costs €16.*

- ***Validation:*** *Remember to validate your Andante card before each journey by scanning it at the yellow machines located in stations or on buses. Failure to do so may result in fines ranging from €120 to €350.*

Exploring Beyond Porto

Port, Railway, Bridge

Porto's transportation network also facilitates easy exploration of nearby attractions and neighboring cities.

- ***Trains:*** *The city's main railway station, São Bento, is a landmark in itself, renowned for its beautiful azulejo tile panels. From here, trains connect to various destinations, including the scenic Douro Valley and* *cities like Braga and Guimarães.*

- ***Buses:*** *Intercity and regional buses operate from Porto, providing access to coastal towns, inland villages, and other Portuguese cities. The Terminal Rodoviário do Campo 24 de Agosto is one of the main bus terminals in the city.*

Tips for Travelers

- ***Peak Hours:*** *Public transportation can be crowded during rush hours (8:00 AM to 9:30 AM and 5:30 PM to 7:00 PM). Planning your travel outside these times can offer a more comfortable experience.*

- ***Accessibility:*** *Most metro stations and many buses are equipped to accommodate passengers with reduced mobility. However, some historic trams may not be accessible.*

- ***Safety:*** *Porto is generally safe, but it's advisable to remain vigilant against pickpockets, especially in crowded areas and on public transportation.*

Aerial View of Porto Riverside and Architecture

Neighborhoods

Ribeira

Ribeira, boats rabelos and Bridge Dom Lui

Walking Through Ribeira

Ribeira is one of the oldest and most vibrant districts in Porto. Nestled along the Douro River, it is a maze of narrow cobblestone streets, colorful houses, and lively squares. The neighborhood carries a deep sense of history, with medieval buildings standing side by side with modern cafés and restaurants. Walking through Ribeira, you will notice traditional azulejo-tiled facades, balconies filled with drying laundry, and locals chatting at small corner shops.

The main square, Praça da Ribeira, is a central gathering spot surrounded by bars and restaurants. It is always buzzing with activity, from street performers entertaining passersby to tourists taking in the river views. Sitting at one of the outdoor terraces here is a great way to soak in the atmosphere while enjoying a glass of vinho verde or a plate of fresh seafood.

Strolling Along Cais da Ribeira

The riverfront promenade, Cais da Ribeira, is one of the most photographed places in Porto. It offers an uninterrupted view of the Dom Luís I Bridge, one of the city's most iconic landmarks. The double-deck iron bridge, designed in the late 19th century, connects Porto with Vila Nova de Gaia, where the famous port wine cellars are located.

From this promenade, you can see the traditional rabelo boats floating along the river. These wooden vessels were once used to transport barrels of wine from the Douro Valley to Porto. Today, they mostly carry visitors on sightseeing cruises. Many companies offer Six Bridges Cruises, which take you along the Douro River, passing under all of Porto's bridges and providing a different perspective of the city. Tickets for these cruises start at €15, with departures every half hour from 10:00 AM to 6:00 PM.

Visiting Historic Landmarks

A short walk from the waterfront brings you to some of Ribeira's most important historical sites. Igreja de São Francisco, one of the most beautiful churches in Porto, is known for its gilded Baroque interior. Nearly every inch of the church's walls and ceilings is covered in gold leaf, creating an overwhelming yet stunning visual effect. Beneath the church, visitors can explore ancient catacombs that hold the remains of Franciscan monks. Entrance costs €7.50, and the church is open daily from 9:00 AM to 7:00 PM.

Nearby is the Palácio da Bolsa, Porto's former stock exchange, which is now a UNESCO-listed building. Its grand interiors, especially the Arab Room, are inspired by Moorish architecture. Guided tours run every day between 9:00 AM and 6:30 PM, with tickets priced at €10.

Another site worth visiting is Casa do Infante, where it is believed that Prince Henry the Navigator was born. Today, it is a museum that tells the story of Porto's maritime history. Entry costs €2.20, and the museum is open from 9:30 AM to 5:30 PM, with a break from 1:00 PM to 2:00 PM.

Dining in Ribeira

Ribeira is one of the best places in Porto to try traditional Portuguese cuisine. Many of the restaurants along the river serve grilled seafood, bacalhau (salted codfish), and francesinha (a meat-filled sandwich covered in melted cheese and beer sauce).

For an authentic dining experience, A Grade is a small, family-run restaurant known for its octopus rice and grilled sardines. It is located on Rua de São Nicolau, open daily from 12:00 PM to 10:00 PM, with main courses averaging €20.

If you are looking for something more upscale, Ribeira Square offers modern takes on classic Portuguese dishes, accompanied by an excellent selection of local wines. The restaurant is located on Praça da Ribeira, open from 12:00 PM to 11:00 PM, with meals costing around €35 per person.

Nightlife and Entertainment

As the sun sets, Ribeira transforms into a lively nightlife spot. Many bars along the river stay open late, serving cocktails, Portuguese wines, and craft beers. Live fado music performances are common, adding to the district's charm. Bar Ponte Pênsil, near the bridge, is a great place to enjoy a drink while admiring Porto's illuminated skyline. Most bars in

Ribeira close around 2:00 AM, though some stay open later on weekends.

Where to Stay

Staying in Ribeira means waking up to some of the best views in Porto. Several boutique hotels and guesthouses offer riverfront accommodations. Pestana Vintage Porto, a five-star hotel set in a historic building, provides luxury rooms overlooking the Douro River. Room rates start at €180 per night.

For a more budget-friendly option, Descobertas Boutique Hotel offers stylish and comfortable rooms just steps from the waterfront. Prices start at €90 per night.

Getting Around

Ribeira is best explored on foot, as most of its streets are narrow and pedestrian-friendly. If you need to get to other parts of Porto, São Bento Train Station is a 10-minute walk away, while the nearest metro stop is at Casa da Música, about 20 minutes away. The area is also served by trams, taxis, and ride-sharing services.

Final Thoughts

Ribeira captures the essence of Porto with its riverfront beauty, historic landmarks, and lively atmosphere. Whether you spend your time wandering through medieval streets, dining on local specialties, or simply sitting by the river watching the boats pass by, this district offers an unforgettable experience.

Scenic View of Porto with Traditional Boat on Douro River

Miragaia

Miragaia, a historic neighborhood in Porto, is characterized by its narrow streets and colorful houses. Walking through its labyrinthine lanes offers a glimpse into the city's past, with traditional architecture and vibrant street life.

Igreja de São Pedro de Miragaia

A notable landmark in the area is the Igreja de São Pedro de Miragaia, an 18th-century church dedicated to the patron saint of fishermen. The church's facade showcases intricate designs that reflect the rich history of the fishing community. Located at Largo de São Pedro de Miragaia, 4050-564 Porto, the church welcomes visitors from Tuesday to Saturday between 3:30 PM and 7:00 PM, and on Sundays from 10:00 AM to 11:30 PM.

Museu Nacional Soares dos Reis

Nearby, the Museu Nacional Soares dos Reis offers a journey through Portuguese art, housing collections that span from the Neolithic period to modern times. Situated in the ancient Carrancas Palace, the museum provides insights into the country's artistic evolution.

Centro Português de Fotografia

For photography enthusiasts, the Centro Português de Fotografia presents exhibitions in a historic setting, offering a unique blend of art and history.

Palácio da Bolsa

Another significant attraction is the Palácio da Bolsa, located at Rua de Ferreira Borges, 4050-253 Porto. This 19th-century neoclassical building, once the city's stock exchange, now hosts guided tours. Visitors can explore its opulent rooms, including the renowned Arab Room, adorned with intricate Moorish-inspired designs. Guided tours are available daily from 9:00 AM to 6:30 PM between April and October, and from 9:00 AM to 12:30 PM and 2:00 PM to 5:30 PM between November and March. Admission is €7.

Exploring Miragaia provides a deeper appreciation of Porto's cultural and historical tapestry, with its blend of architectural gems and artistic venues.

Porto's vibrant art scene is showcased through its diverse museums and galleries, each offering unique insights into the city's rich cultural heritage.

Serralves Museum of Contemporary Art

The Serralves Museum of Contemporary Art stands as a beacon for modern art enthusiasts. Designed by architect

Álvaro Siza Vieira, the museum is nestled within the expansive Parque de Serralves. Visitors can explore rotating exhibitions featuring both Portuguese and international artists. The museum is located at Rua Dom João de Castro, 210, 4150-417 Porto. Operating hours are from 10:00 AM to 7:00 PM, with extended hours on weekends. Admission fees vary depending on the exhibitions.

Museu Nacional Soares dos Reis

As Portugal's oldest public art museum, the Museu Nacional Soares dos Reis offers a comprehensive collection of Portuguese art. Housed in the Carrancas Palace, the museum showcases works from the Neolithic period to the 20th century, including notable sculptures and paintings. The museum is situated at Rua de Dom Manuel II, 44, 4050-522 Porto. It operates from 10:00 AM to 6:00 PM, Tuesday through Sunday. Admission is €5, with free entry on Sundays until 2:00 PM.

Centro Português de Fotografia

For photography aficionados, the Centro Português de Fotografia provides a captivating experience. Located in a former prison, the center features exhibitions that highlight both historical and contemporary photography. The building itself adds a unique dimension to the visit, blending architectural history with visual art. Found at Largo Amor de Perdição, 4050-008 Porto, the center is open from 10:00 AM to 6:00 PM, Tuesday to Sunday, and admission is free.

Museu de Arte Contemporânea da Fundação de Serralves

Another gem in Porto's art scene is the Museu de Arte Contemporânea da Fundação de Serralves. This museum offers a diverse collection of contemporary art and is set within a beautifully landscaped park, providing a serene environment for art appreciation. The museum is located at Rua Dom João de Castro, 210, 4150-417 Porto. It welcomes visitors from 10:00 AM to 7:00 PM, with extended hours on weekends. Admission fees vary depending on the exhibitions.

These institutions collectively enrich Porto's cultural landscape, offering residents and visitors alike opportunities to engage with art and history.

Cedofeita

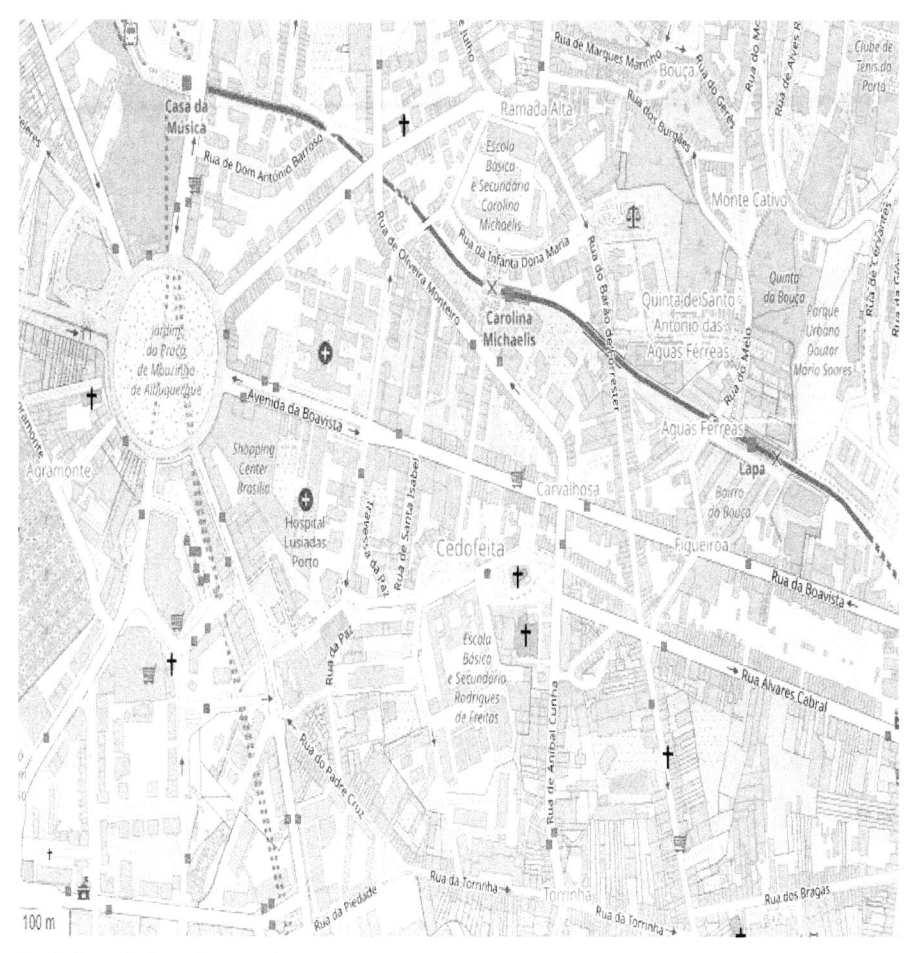

Cedofeita | OpenStreetMap

Carlos Alberto Square in Cedofeita

Cedofeita is a vibrant neighborhood in Porto that harmoniously blends traditional charm with contemporary flair. Its streets are lined with historic architecture, modern art galleries, and a variety of dining establishments, making it a dynamic area for visitors.

Rua de Cedofeita

The main artery of the neighborhood, Rua de Cedofeita, is a bustling pedestrian street renowned for its diverse shopping options. Here, visitors can explore a mix of traditional shops and international brand stores, offering everything from local crafts to fashion. The street is also dotted with cozy cafés, providing perfect spots to relax and people-watch.

Rua de Miguel Bombarda

Art enthusiasts will find Rua de Miguel Bombarda particularly appealing. This street is the epicenter of Porto's contemporary art scene, hosting numerous galleries that showcase works from emerging and established artists. The area frequently holds "Bombarda Art Block" events, where galleries simultaneously inaugurate new exhibitions, creating a vibrant cultural atmosphere.

Dining in Cedofeita

Cedofeita boasts a rich culinary landscape. From traditional Portuguese eateries to international cuisine, the neighborhood caters to diverse palates. Whether you're craving local specialties or contemporary fusion dishes, the area's restaurants and cafés offer a variety of options to satisfy your taste buds.

Accommodation in Cedofeita

For those looking to stay in Cedofeita, the neighborhood offers a range of accommodations. From boutique hotels to guesthouses, visitors can find lodging that suits their *preferences and budget, all while being immersed in the local culture.*

Cedofeita's unique blend of art, commerce, and gastronomy makes it a must-visit destination for anyone exploring Porto.

For a visual tour of Cedofeita, you might find the following video insightful:

Boavista

Boavista

Exploring Avenida da Boavista

Boavista is one of the most dynamic districts in Porto, blending modern architecture, cultural landmarks, and vibrant city life. Avenida da Boavista, the longest avenue in the city, stretches for 5.5 kilometers, linking the historic center to the Atlantic coast. This wide boulevard is home to high-end designer stores, corporate buildings, luxury hotels, and some of Porto's most important attractions. The avenue is always busy, with locals commuting for work, shoppers browsing upscale boutiques, and visitors exploring the area's cultural highlights.

Rotunda da Boavista and the Peninsular War Monument

At the center of Boavista, Rotunda da Boavista, a large roundabout officially named Praça de Mouzinho de Albuquerque, is a major landmark. It is hard to miss the towering Peninsular War Monument, which commemorates Portugal's resistance against Napoleon's forces in the early 19th century. The monument features a striking bronze lion crushing a French eagle, symbolizing the victory of the Portuguese and British allies over the invading troops. Surrounding the monument is a beautifully landscaped park with benches, fountains, and walking paths. Locals often gather here to relax, and the green space offers a peaceful break from the urban surroundings.

Casa da Música

Right next to Rotunda da Boavista is one of Porto's most iconic buildings, Casa da Música. Designed by Dutch architect Rem Koolhaas, this state-of-the-art concert hall stands out with its bold, geometric shape and futuristic glass windows. It hosts a variety of performances, from classical and jazz to electronic and experimental music. Guided tours allow visitors to explore its unique design and understand the thought process behind its acoustics. The building also has a rooftop terrace with panoramic views of Porto.

Casa da Música is open daily from 10:00 AM to 6:00 PM, with extended hours on concert nights. Guided tours cost €10 per person, while concert ticket prices range from €10 to €50, depending on the event. The box office is located inside the building, and there is also a café where visitors can enjoy a meal or drink before a show.

Serralves Museum and Park

A short drive from Boavista, the Serralves Museum of Contemporary Art is one of Portugal's most important cultural institutions. The museum is housed in a minimalist, modernist building and features rotating exhibitions from both Portuguese and international artists. Surrounding the museum is Serralves Park, a massive green space with beautifully manicured gardens, outdoor sculptures, and a treetop walk that offers a different perspective of the landscape. Visitors can also explore the Serralves Villa, a stunning Art Deco mansion inside the park.

The museum and park are open from 10:00 AM to 7:00 PM, with extended hours on weekends. Admission is €12 per person, with discounts available for students and seniors. The site also features a café with a terrace overlooking the gardens, making it a perfect place to unwind after exploring the exhibits.

Parque da Cidade

For those looking to escape the city's hustle, Parque da Cidade is the perfect spot. As Porto's largest urban park, covering 83 hectares, it offers walking and cycling trails, small lakes, and picnic areas. The park extends all the way to the coastline, meaning visitors can take a leisurely stroll from the city to the beachfront promenade in Foz do Douro. It is a popular place for locals to exercise, walk their dogs, or simply enjoy the fresh air. Unlike some parks in Porto, this one is free to enter and is open daily from 7:00 AM to 10:00 PM.

Dining in Boavista

Boavista's dining scene is as diverse as the district itself, offering everything from trendy brunch spots to traditional Portuguese restaurants. Negra Café Boavista, located on Rua de 5 de Outubro, is a stylish café known for its smoothie bowls, fresh pastries, and gourmet coffee. It is a popular place for both locals and visitors, especially in the mornings. The café is open daily from 9:00 AM to 7:00 PM, with an average meal price of €15.

For those wanting to try authentic Portuguese grilled dishes, Churrasqueira Rotunda Boavista is a great choice. Located on Avenida da Boavista, it serves grilled sea bass, piri-piri chicken, and hearty Portuguese stews. The atmosphere is casual, and the food is always fresh. The restaurant is open from 12:00 PM to 10:00 PM, with main courses averaging €12.

For Italian food lovers, Pizzaria Luzzo Boavista offers wood-fired pizzas with a modern twist. Located on Rua de Pedro Hispano, it is a cozy spot with a great selection of toppings and house-made dough. The restaurant is open from 12:00 PM to 11:00 PM, and pizzas cost around €14.

Where to Stay

Boavista is home to several high-end hotels that cater to both business and leisure travelers. Porto Palácio Hotel, located on Avenida da Boavista, is a five-star property offering luxury rooms, a rooftop bar, a spa, and a fine-dining restaurant. The hotel provides excellent service and stunning views of the city. Room rates start at €120 per night.

For a more affordable but equally stylish stay, BessaHotel Boavista is a popular option. Located on Rua Dr. Marques de Carvalho, this four-star hotel features modern rooms, a fitness center, and an on-site restaurant. The atmosphere is contemporary and welcoming, making it a great choice for those looking for comfort without overspending. Room rates start at €90 per night.

Getting Around

Boavista is well-connected by Porto's metro and bus network, making it easy to navigate. Casa da Música metro station is a central hub, offering quick connections to the historic center, the airport, and other districts. Several bus lines run along Avenida da Boavista, providing additional transportation options. The district is also pedestrian-friendly, especially around the Rotunda and Casa da Música, where wide sidewalks make walking enjoyable. Taxis and ride-sharing services are widely available, and for those wanting to explore at their own pace, bike rentals are another good option.

Final Thoughts

Boavista is a district that balances tradition and modernity, making it one of Porto's most exciting areas to explore. Whether you are attending a concert at Casa da Música, strolling through Serralves Park, or enjoying a meal in one of the many restaurants, there is something for every type of traveler. The neighborhood's strategic location, between the city center and the coast, makes it a great place to stay and experience both sides of Porto.

Foz

Foz do Douro, commonly referred to as Foz, is a picturesque district in Porto where the Douro River meets the Atlantic Ocean. This area is renowned for its scenic beauty, blending golden beaches with historic landmarks, making it a must-visit for those exploring Porto.

Scenic Promenades

One of Foz's main attractions is its extensive promenade, ideal for leisurely walks along the waterfront. The esplanade stretches from the Jardim do Passeio Alegre to the Castelo do Queijo, offering stunning ocean views and a refreshing sea breeze. Along the way, you'll encounter several beaches, such as Praia dos Ingleses and Praia da Luz, each providing unique coastal experiences.

Historic Fortresses

Foz is home to two notable forts that once guarded the entrance to the Douro River. The São João da Foz Fortress, dating back to the 16th century, stands as a testament to the area's strategic importance. Similarly, the Castelo do Queijo, perched along the coastline, offers insights into Portugal's maritime defenses and provides panoramic views of the Atlantic.

Mercado da Foz

For a taste of local life, a visit to Mercado da Foz is essential. This market hall offers fresh produce, seafood, and traditional Portuguese delicacies. It's an excellent spot to sample regional specialties and experience the community's daily rhythm.

Transportation to Foz

Reaching Foz from central Porto is both scenic and straightforward. The historic tram number 1 departs from the Infante stop near São Francisco's Church and travels along the riverbank, arriving in Foz in approximately 20 minutes. This journey not only provides convenient access but also offers picturesque views of the Douro River along the way.

Foz encapsulates the serene coastal charm of Porto, combining natural beauty with cultural landmarks. Whether you're interested in sunbathing on its beaches, exploring historic sites, or indulging in local cuisine, Foz offers a diverse array of experiences that cater to all visitors.

Gaia

Vila Nova de Gaia, commonly known as Gaia, is situated directly across the Douro River from Porto. This city is renowned for its port wine cellars, scenic riverfront, and expansive beaches, offering a diverse range of experiences for visitors.

Port Wine Cellars

Gaia is synonymous with port wine. The city's riverside is lined with historic cellars where this fortified wine has been aged for centuries. Notable cellars include Graham's, Taylor's, and Sandeman, each offering guided tours and tastings. These tours provide insights into the wine-making process and the rich history of port wine.

Cais de Gaia

The Cais de Gaia is a lively promenade along the Douro River, offering stunning views of Porto's Ribeira district. Lined with restaurants, cafés, and bars, it's an ideal spot to savor local cuisine while enjoying the picturesque scenery. Street performers and market stalls add to the vibrant atmosphere, making it a popular gathering place for both locals and tourists.

Teleférico de Gaia

For a unique perspective of the area, the Teleférico de Gaia cable car transports visitors from the riverbank to the upper levels of Gaia. This short ride offers panoramic views of the Douro River, the iconic Dom Luís I Bridge, and the historic centers of both Gaia and Porto.

Beaches of Gaia

Beyond its urban attractions, Gaia boasts a coastline with several Blue Flag beaches. Beaches such as Praia da Madalena and Praia de Miramar are known for their clean sands and excellent facilities, providing a relaxing escape from the city's hustle and bustle.

Monastery of Serra do Pilar

Perched atop a hill, the Monastery of Serra do Pilar is a 17th-century monastery offering breathtaking views of Porto and the Douro River. Its unique circular church and cloister are architectural highlights, and the site is recognized as a UNESCO World Heritage site.

Vila Nova de Gaia seamlessly blends cultural heritage with natural beauty. Whether you're exploring historic wine cellars, strolling along the riverfront, or relaxing on its beaches, Gaia offers a rich and diverse experience that complements any visit to the Porto region.

Culture

Traditions

Porto, Portugal's second-largest city, is a vibrant tapestry of traditions that reflect its rich cultural heritage. Among these, the São João Festival stands out as a highlight of the city's festive calendar.

São João Festival

Celebrated annually on June 23rd, the São João Festival is a lively event where locals and visitors take to the streets to honor Saint John. The festivities include unique customs such as gently tapping others on the head with plastic hammers and releasing illuminated hot air balloons into the night sky. Grilled sardines are a culinary staple during this celebration, with street vendors and restaurants offering this traditional dish to revelers.

Rabelo Boats

Porto's identity is closely linked to the Douro River and its traditional rabelo boats. Historically, these wooden vessels transported port wine barrels from the Douro Valley vineyards to the cellars in Vila Nova de Gaia. Today, they symbolize the city's maritime heritage and are prominently featured during festivals and river tours.

Fado Music

Fado, a soulful genre of Portuguese music, holds a special place in Porto's cultural scene. Characterized by melancholic melodies and expressive lyrics, fado performances can be experienced in various venues throughout the city, offering insight into Portugal's musical traditions.

Porto's museums and galleries offer a rich exploration of its artistic and cultural heritage.

Museu Nacional Soares dos Reis

As Portugal's oldest public museum, the Museu Nacional Soares dos Reis houses an extensive collection of Portuguese art, including sculptures, paintings, and decorative arts from the 19th and 20th centuries. Located at Rua de Dom Manuel II 44, 4050-522 Porto, the museum operates from 10:00 AM to 6:00 PM, Tuesday through Sunday. Admission is €5, with free entry on Sundays until 2:00 PM.

Serralves Museum of Contemporary Art

The Serralves Museum of Contemporary Art is a leading institution showcasing contemporary art within a minimalist building designed by Álvaro Siza Vieira. Situated at Rua Dom João de Castro 210, 4150-417 Porto, the museum is open from 10:00 AM to 7:00 PM, with extended hours on weekends. Admission fees vary depending on the exhibitions.

World of Wine (WoW)

Located in Vila Nova de Gaia, the World of Wine is a cultural district dedicated to the region's wine heritage. It features interactive exhibits, wine tasting experiences, restaurants, and shops. Opening hours and admission prices vary by exhibit and experience.

These institutions and traditions provide a deep dive into Porto's cultural fabric, offering visitors a comprehensive understanding of the city's artistic and historical significance.

Language

The Portuguese Language in Porto

Portuguese is the official language spoken in Porto, as it is throughout Portugal. The language has Latin roots, influenced by centuries of cultural and historical exchanges. In Porto, the local accent is distinct from the one spoken in Lisbon, with a stronger and more pronounced pronunciation.

Commonly Spoken Languages

While Portuguese is the primary language, English is widely understood, especially in tourist areas, restaurants, hotels, and museums. Many younger people and those working in the tourism industry speak fluent English. Spanish is also understood by some locals due to linguistic similarities, though many prefer to communicate in Portuguese rather than Spanish. French is spoken by some older residents who learned it in school, and German is occasionally heard in tourist areas.

Useful Portuguese Phrases for Visitors

When visiting Porto, learning a few basic Portuguese phrases can enhance your experience and show respect for the local culture. Some useful phrases include:

Olá – Hello

Obrigado (if male) / Obrigada (if female) – Thank you

Por favor – Please

Quanto custa? – How much does it cost?

Fala inglês? – Do you speak English?

Desculpe – Excuse me / Sorry

Onde fica…? – Where is…?

Pode ajudar-me? – Can you help me?

Language in Public Spaces

Most street signs, menus, and public transport information are in Portuguese, but in major tourist areas, English translations are often available. Museums, galleries, and attractions usually provide information in multiple languages, including English, Spanish, and French. Some guided tours offer multilingual options.

Understanding Local Expressions

Porto residents, known as "tripeiros," have unique expressions and slang that may differ from standard

Portuguese. Locals may use informal greetings like "Então, tudo bem?" meaning "So, everything good?" and phrases such as "fixe" to say something is cool.

Language Barriers and Tips

Even though many people in Porto speak English, some smaller local businesses, markets, and traditional restaurants may only communicate in Portuguese. Using translation apps or carrying a small phrasebook can be helpful in these situations. Showing effort by using simple Portuguese words is often appreciated by locals, even if your pronunciation is not perfect.

Portugal, Porto, Church

Festivals

São João Festival

The most famous festival in Porto is the São João Festival, held annually on the night of June 23rd. It is one of the largest street celebrations in Portugal, honoring Saint John the Baptist. Throughout the evening, the city fills with music, dancing, fireworks, and traditional food. A unique tradition of this festival is hitting people on the head with plastic hammers or waving garlic flowers, a playful custom meant to bring good luck. Grilled sardines, caldo verde (Portuguese cabbage soup), and bifanas (pork sandwiches) are staple foods during the festivities. The celebration reaches its peak at midnight with a massive fireworks display over the Douro River, followed by thousands of people walking to Foz do Douro to watch the sunrise.

Fantasporto

Fantasporto is Porto's International Film Festival, focusing on fantasy, horror, and science fiction films. It is one of the most recognized film festivals in Europe and attracts filmmakers and movie lovers from around the world. The festival takes place every February or March, screening a mix of independent films, international blockbusters, and experimental cinema. Screenings are held at the Teatro Rivoli, *with tickets varying depending on the session and film category.*

Festa de Nossa Senhora da Agonia

While primarily celebrated in Viana do Castelo, this religious festival also has events in Porto. Taking place in mid-August, it honors the patron saint of fishermen, featuring processions, folk music, traditional costumes, and fireworks. The festival showcases Portugal's deep maritime heritage and faith.

Queima das Fitas

Queima das Fitas, or the "Burning of the Ribbons," is Porto's student festival, celebrated in May by university students. It marks the end of the academic year and includes a parade, concerts, and traditional student rituals. Participants wear colored ribbons and academic robes while taking part in the celebrations, which last for an entire week. The event is particularly lively at Queimódromo, a dedicated festival area where major concerts take place.

Festa de São Pedro

This festival, dedicated to Saint Peter, is celebrated in late June in nearby coastal towns such as Póvoa de Varzim and Vila Nova de Gaia. However, Porto also hosts festivities with traditional dancing, music, and grilled sardines. Saint Peter is the patron saint of fishermen, so many events take place along the river and the coast.

Porto Book Fair

Porto hosts an annual book fair, Feira do Livro do Porto, which takes place in August or September at the Palácio de Cristal Gardens. This literary event attracts authors, publishers, and book lovers, offering book signings, readings, and cultural discussions. The setting in the gardens provides a relaxed environment for visitors to browse books and enjoy views of the Douro River.

Christmas and New Year's Eve Celebrations

During December, Porto transforms with Christmas lights, markets, and festive decorations. The main Christmas market is held at Praça da Batalha, featuring handmade crafts, seasonal treats, and holiday music. On New Year's Eve, Avenida dos Aliados becomes the center of celebrations, with a large fireworks show and live music performances. Many people also gather along the riverfront in Ribeira and Vila Nova de Gaia to watch the fireworks over the Douro.

Mercado da Alegria

The Mercado da Alegria, or "Market of Joy," is a traditional fair held several times a year, offering handmade goods, traditional Portuguese products, and local delicacies. It is a great opportunity to experience Porto's artisan culture and shop for authentic souvenirs.

Festa do Vinho Verde e dos Petiscos

This festival celebrates vinho verde, Portugal's famous green wine, along with traditional petiscos (small Portuguese tapas). Hosted in Porto and surrounding areas, the event allows visitors to sample different varieties of vinho verde while enjoying regional snacks such as cured meats, cheeses, and seafood. It is a popular event for both locals and tourists who want to explore Portuguese gastronomy.

Festival Marés Vivas

Festival Marés Vivas is one of northern Portugal's biggest music festivals, held every summer in Vila Nova de Gaia. It features both international and Portuguese artists across various genres, attracting thousands of music lovers. The festival grounds are located near the beach, providing a unique setting for live performances. Ticket prices vary depending on the lineup and festival duration.

Porto Wine Fest

Held in Vila Nova de Gaia, Porto Wine Fest is dedicated to Portugal's famous port wine. The event brings together wine producers, sommeliers, and enthusiasts for tastings, workshops, and pairings with Portuguese cuisine. Visitors can sample different styles of port, from ruby and tawny to vintage selections, while enjoying views of the Douro River.

Festa do Senhor de Matosinhos

Taking place in Matosinhos, a coastal city just outside Porto, this festival blends religious devotion with lively entertainment. It is held in May and includes processions, traditional fairs, fireworks, and a variety of food stalls selling grilled seafood and local pastries. The festival is known for its impressive street decorations and carnival rides, making it a favorite among families.

Monuments

Porto, Portugal's second-largest city, is rich in history and culture, boasting numerous monuments that reflect its diverse architectural heritage. Exploring these landmarks offers insight into the city's past and its evolution over the centuries.

Porto Cathedral (Sé do Porto)

Perched atop the Pena Ventosa hill, the Porto Cathedral is one of the city's oldest and most significant monuments. Its construction began in the 12th century, showcasing

Romanesque architecture, with later Baroque and Gothic additions. Visitors can admire its impressive façade, the beautiful rose window, and the cloisters adorned with traditional azulejos (blue and white tiles). The cathedral is located at Terreiro da Sé, 4050-573 Porto, and is open daily from 9:00 AM to 6:30 PM. Admission is free, but access to the cloisters requires a fee of €3.

Clérigos Tower (Torre dos Clérigos)

A defining feature of Porto's skyline, the Clérigos Tower stands at 75 meters and offers panoramic views of the city. Designed by Italian architect Nicolau Nasoni in the 18th century, this Baroque masterpiece is part of the Clérigos Church complex. Visitors can climb its 225 steps to enjoy breathtaking vistas. The tower is situated at Rua de São Filipe de Nery, 4050-546 Porto, and is open daily from 9:00 AM to 7:00 PM. Entrance costs €5, which includes access to the church and museum.

São Bento Railway Station

More than just a transportation hub, São Bento Railway Station is renowned for its stunning azulejo panels. Completed in 1916, the station's entrance hall features over 20,000 tiles depicting significant events in Portuguese history, crafted by

74

artist Jorge Colaço. Located at Praça de Almeida Garrett, 4000-069 Porto, the station is open daily, and entry is free.

Palácio da Bolsa (Stock Exchange Palace)

Constructed in the 19th century, the Palácio da Bolsa reflects Porto's mercantile prosperity. This neoclassical building features opulent rooms, such as the Arab Room, inspired by the Alhambra Palace in Granada. Guided tours are available to explore its rich interiors. The palace is located at Rua de Ferreira Borges, 4050-253 Porto, and is open daily from 9:00 AM to 6:30 PM. Admission is €10, with guided tours offered in multiple languages.

Church of São Francisco (Igreja de São Francisco)

Behind its modest Gothic exterior, the Church of São Francisco dazzles visitors with its lavish Baroque interior, adorned with intricate wood carvings covered in gold leaf. The church also houses a museum in its former cloisters. Located at Rua do Infante Dom Henrique, 4050-297 Porto, it is open daily from 9:00 AM to 7:00 PM. Entrance costs €7.50, which includes access to the museum and catacombs.

Dom Luís I Bridge

Spanning the Douro River, the Dom Luís I Bridge is an iconic symbol of Porto. Completed in 1886 and designed by engineer

Théophile Seyrig, a disciple of Gustave Eiffel, the double-deck iron bridge connects Porto to Vila Nova de Gaia. Pedestrians can cross the upper deck alongside the metro line, enjoying stunning views of the river and cityscape. Access to the bridge is free and available at all times.

Monument to the Heroes of the Peninsular War

Situated in the Rotunda da Boavista (Boavista Roundabout), this monument commemorates the Portuguese soldiers who fought in the Peninsular War against Napoleon's forces. Unveiled in 1952, the centerpiece is a 45-meter-high column topped by a lion (symbolizing Portugal) dominating an eagle (representing France). The base features sculptures depicting scenes from the war. The monument is accessible to the public at all times and is free to visit.

Museums

Porto boasts a rich tapestry of museums and galleries that reflect its vibrant cultural heritage. Here's a curated selection of some noteworthy institutions:

Museu Nacional Soares dos Reis

As Portugal's oldest public museum, the Museu Nacional Soares dos Reis offers an extensive collection of Portuguese art, including sculptures, paintings, and decorative arts from the 19th and 20th centuries. Located at Rua de Dom Manuel II 56, 4050-522 Porto, the museum operates from 10:00 AM to 6:00 PM, Tuesday through Sunday. Admission is €5, with free entry on Sundays until 2:00 PM.

Serralves Museum of Contemporary Art

The Serralves Museum of Contemporary Art is a leading institution showcasing contemporary art within a minimalist building designed by Álvaro Siza Vieira. Situated at Rua Dom João de Castro 210, 4150-417 Porto, the museum is open from 10:00 AM to 7:00 PM, with extended hours on weekends. Admission fees vary depending on the exhibitions.

World of Wine (WoW)

Located in Vila Nova de Gaia, the World of Wine is a cultural district dedicated to the region's wine heritage. It features interactive exhibits, wine tasting experiences, restaurants, and shops. Opening hours and admission prices vary by exhibit and experience.

FC Porto Museum

Football enthusiasts can explore the history of FC Porto at the FC Porto Museum, which showcases trophies, memorabilia, and interactive exhibits. Situated at Estádio do Dragão, Via Futebol Clube do Porto, 4350-415 Porto, the museum is open daily from 10:00 AM to 7:00 PM. Admission is €12, with discounts available for children and seniors.

Casa do Infante

Casa do Infante, believed to be the birthplace of Prince Henry the Navigator, houses archaeological findings and exhibits detailing Porto's history. Located at Rua da Alfândega 10, 4050-029 Porto, it operates from 9:30 AM to 6:00 PM, Tuesday to Sunday. Admission is €2.20, with free entry on weekends and public holidays.

Outdoor

Cruises

Porto offers a variety of river cruises that allow visitors to experience the city's beauty from the Douro River. One popular option is the 6 Bridges Cruise, a 50-minute journey aboard a traditional Rabelo boat. This cruise provides views of Porto and Vila Nova de Gaia's riverbanks and their six connecting bridges. Prices are appealing, and online bookings often come with a 10% discount.

For a more immersive experience, full-day cruises into the Douro Valley are available. These typically include lunch and wine tasting, offering a comprehensive exploration of the region's landscapes and culinary delights. Prices for such tours start around $100 per person.

Another option is the Douro River day cruise, which often includes visits to local wineries and picturesque villages. These cruises provide a deeper insight into the region's culture and history. Prices and durations vary, with some tours starting at $50 for shorter experiences.

For those seeking a luxurious experience, companies like Riviera River Cruises offer 8-day journeys along the Douro River, starting from $2,649 per person. These cruises often include excursions to historic sites, gourmet dining, and onboard entertainment.

Most cruises depart from the Ribeira or Vila Nova de Gaia waterfronts. It's advisable to check the specific departure points and times when booking. Operating hours and availability can vary, so advance reservations are recommended to ensure a spot on your preferred cruise.

Embarking on a river cruise in Porto is a memorable way to appreciate the city's architecture, culture, and the scenic beauty of the Douro Valley.

Gardens

Porto boasts a variety of gardens that offer both locals and visitors serene escapes amidst the city's vibrant atmosphere.

Jardins do Palácio de Cristal (Crystal Palace Gardens)

Designed in the 19th century by German landscape architect Émile David, the Crystal Palace Gardens span nearly 20 acres on the western edge of Porto's city center. These romantic gardens are renowned for their winding paths, diverse plant species, and breathtaking views of the Douro River. Visitors can also encounter peacocks and chickens roaming freely, adding to the gardens' charm.

Jardim Botânico do Porto (Porto Botanical Garden)

Located at Rua do Campo Alegre 1191, the Porto Botanical Garden is managed by the University of Porto. It features a diverse collection of approximately 1,300 plant species, organized into thematic sections such as camellias, native plants, cacti, succulents, rhododendrons, and conifers. The garden also includes historical elements like the Rose Garden, the J Letter Garden, and the Fish Garden, separated by Camellia japonica hedges.

Parque de Serralves (Serralves Park)

Adjacent to the Serralves Museum of Contemporary Art, Serralves Park encompasses 18 hectares of meticulously designed landscapes. Influenced by French garden design, the park features romantic gardens, a rose garden, woodlands, and meadows. The art-deco style Serralves Villa adds to the park's aesthetic appeal.

Jardim do Passeio Alegre

Situated at the mouth of the Douro River in the Foz do Douro district, Jardim do Passeio Alegre is a historic garden adorned with palm trees, fountains, and traditional Portuguese tilework (azulejos). The garden's location offers scenic views of the river meeting the Atlantic Ocean, making it a popular spot for leisurely strolls.

Jardim das Virtudes

Jardim das Virtudes is a terraced garden offering panoramic views of the Douro River and Vila Nova de Gaia. Its unique vertical layout, with cascading terraces, provides visitors with various vantage points to appreciate the surrounding landscape.

Beaches

Porto offers a variety of beaches that cater to different preferences, from bustling urban shores to serene coastal retreats. Here's an overview of some notable beaches in and around Porto:

Praia de Matosinhos

Located to the northwest of Porto's city center, Praia de Matosinhos is a favorite among locals and tourists alike. Its expansive stretch of golden sand and consistent waves make it

ideal for surfing enthusiasts. The beach is easily accessible via public transportation, with the Matosinhos Sul metro station just a short walk away. Along the promenade, visitors can find numerous seafood restaurants offering fresh catches of the day. There is no entrance fee to the beach, and it is open year-round.

Praia dos Ingleses

Situated in the Foz do Douro district, Praia dos Ingleses is known for its picturesque setting and tranquil atmosphere. The beach features a mix of sand and rocky formations, providing a unique landscape for visitors. It's a popular spot for those looking to relax and enjoy the sunset. Nearby, there are several cafés and bars where one can savor local delicacies. Access to the beach is free, and it remains open throughout the year.

Praia da Aguda

Located approximately 13 kilometers south of Porto, Praia da Aguda is a charming fishing village beach known for its wide sandy shore and rich marine life. The beach is recognized as a Blue Flag beach, indicating high environmental and quality standards. Visitors can explore the local fish market or dine at nearby seafood restaurants. The beach is accessible by train from Porto, with Aguda station being a short walk away. There is no entrance fee, and it is open all year.

Praia da Sereia (Mermaid Beach)

Situated in Vila Nova de Gaia, just south of Porto, Praia da Sereia offers a serene environment with sand dunes and small beach huts. The laid-back atmosphere and manageable crowds make it an ideal spot for relaxation. The beach is easily reachable via public transportation, taking about 20 minutes from Porto's city center. Access to the beach is free, and it is open year-round.

Praia do Senhor da Pedra

This beach is renowned for the Senhor da Pedra chapel, a picturesque 17th-century structure perched on a rocky outcrop by the sea. The unique blend of cultural heritage and natural beauty makes it a must-visit destination. The beach is located in Vila Nova de Gaia and is accessible via train to Miramar station, followed by a short walk. There is no entrance fee, and it remains open throughout the year.

Hiking

Porto and its surrounding regions offer a variety of hiking opportunities that cater to both casual walkers and seasoned trekkers. Here are some notable trails and areas to explore:

Serras do Porto Park

Located east of Porto, the Serras do Porto Park spans approximately 5,974 hectares and encompasses parts of Gondomar, Paredes, and Valongo. Established in 2017, this protected landscape features ancient geological formations and diverse ecosystems. The park offers several marked trails, such as the GR Serras do Porto and PR Trilho dos Romanos, guiding hikers through forests, valleys, and historical sites. Access to the park is free, and it remains open year-round.

Passadiços do Paiva (Paiva Walkways)

Situated about an hour's drive from Porto, the Paiva Walkways offer an 8-kilometer wooden pathway along the Paiva River. This trail provides stunning views of waterfalls, quartz crystal formations, and rich biodiversity. It's suitable for most fitness levels, though some sections include steep stairs. The walk typically takes 2 to 3 hours to complete. Tickets cost €1 during weekdays and €2 on weekends and holidays. It's advisable to book in advance, especially during peak seasons.

Peneda-Gerês National Park

As Portugal's only national park, Peneda-Gerês is located about 100 kilometers northeast of Porto. The park boasts a variety of hiking trails that traverse dense forests, granite peaks, and traditional villages. Trails range from short walks to multi-day treks, catering to various skill levels. Entrance to the park is free, but guided tours may incur additional costs. The park is accessible year-round, though spring and autumn offer milder weather conditions.

Serra da Freita

Approximately 70 kilometers southeast of Porto, Serra da Freita is known for its unique geological formations, including the Pedras Parideiras (birthing stones) and the impressive Frecha da Mizarela waterfall, one of Europe's highest with a 75-meter drop. Hiking trails in this area vary in difficulty and length, guiding visitors through scenic landscapes and quaint villages. Access to the trails is free, and they are open throughout the year.

Douro Valley

The Douro Valley, renowned for its terraced vineyards and the Douro River, offers picturesque hiking opportunities. Trails wind through vineyards, olive groves, and almond orchards, providing panoramic views of the valley. Some routes include visits to local quintas (wine estates) for wine tastings. While many trails are free to access, guided hikes or wine tastings may involve additional costs. The best times to hike are during spring and autumn when the weather is pleasant, and the landscapes are vibrant.

Before setting out, it's recommended to check trail conditions, carry sufficient water, wear appropriate footwear, and inform someone of your itinerary. Whether you're seeking a leisurely walk or a challenging trek, the Porto region offers diverse hiking experiences that showcase its natural beauty and cultural heritage.

Cycling

Porto offers a variety of cycling experiences, from scenic coastal paths to urban explorations. Here's a guide to help you navigate the city's cycling landscape:

Cycling Routes in Porto

Coastal Pathways: *On the southern side of the Douro River, there are miles of coastal cycle paths. These traffic-free lanes start on the riverfront west of the Port lodges, beyond the Ponte da Arrábida bridge by the pleasant marina area. The path follows the Douro River into its estuary and nature reserve before turning south to follow the coast. The cycle paths run more or less unbroken for 20 km, all the way to Espinho on roadside cycle paths or wooden beach boardwalks.*

Urban Trails: *Porto's city center features several well-indicated bike routes, including paths running along the Atlantic Ocean and the Foz do Douro River.*

Bike Rentals in Porto

Biclas & Triclas: Located in Porto, this rental service offers city bikes at rates starting from €7 for 2 hours, up to €19 for a 24-hour period. They provide helmets, integrated locks, and optional rear bags for an additional €3 per day.

Vieguini: As Porto's first bike and scooter rental shop, Vieguini offers a range of bicycles with competitive pricing and quality service. They also provide insights into the best routes and attractions in the city.

Porto Rent a Bike: This service offers a wide range of bikes, including electric and mountain bikes, with rental options by the hour, day, or week. They also provide customized routes to help you explore the best of Porto.

Guided Cycling Tours

Baja Bikes: Offering guided bike tours, Baja Bikes provides an excellent way to explore Porto's highlights while learning about its history and culture.

Komoot: For self-guided experiences, Komoot offers detailed cycling routes in Porto, such as the circular route from Porto *to Matosinhos and the Vila Nova de Gaia and its beaches route.*

Food

Dishes

Porto's culinary scene is rich and diverse, offering visitors a chance to indulge in traditional dishes that reflect the city's history and culture. Here are some must-try dishes:

Francesinha

This iconic sandwich is a Porto staple. It consists of layers of bread filled with wet-cured ham, linguiça (a type of Portuguese sausage), fresh sausage like chipolata, and steak or roast meat. The sandwich is then covered with melted cheese and drenched in a spiced tomato-and-beer sauce. Typically served with french fries, it's a hearty meal that showcases the city's love for robust flavors.

Tripas à Moda do Porto

A dish deeply rooted in Porto's history, Tripas à Moda do Porto is a tripe stew made with white beans, carrots, and rice. This traditional meal reflects the city's nickname "tripeiros," originating from the 15th century when residents sacrificed meat for explorers, consuming tripe instead.

Bacalhau à Gomes de Sá

A beloved Portuguese dish, Bacalhau à Gomes de Sá is a casserole featuring salted cod, potatoes, onions, eggs, and olives. Baked to perfection, it offers a harmonious blend of flavors that epitomize comfort food.

Bolinhos de Bacalhau

These deep-fried codfish cakes are a popular snack or appetizer. Made from a mixture of salted cod, mashed potatoes, and fresh herbs, they're crispy on the outside and tender inside, often enjoyed with a squeeze of lemon.

Alheira

Alheira is a unique Portuguese sausage traditionally made from a mix of meats, excluding pork, and bread. Often served fried or baked, it's accompanied by french fries, rice, and a fried egg, offering a flavorful experience distinct from typical sausages.

Exploring these dishes provides a delicious insight into Porto's rich culinary heritage, ensuring a memorable gastronomic journey.

Restaurants

Porto, Flow, Meal

Porto's culinary scene is rich and diverse, offering a range of dining experiences from traditional Portuguese fare to innovative contemporary cuisine. Here are some notable restaurants to consider:

Casa Guedes Tradicional

Renowned for its succulent pork sandwiches, Casa Guedes has become a local favorite. The tender pork is complemented by a variety of accompaniments, making it a must-try for visitors seeking authentic flavors. Located at Praça dos Poveiros 130, this eatery offers a casual dining experience with prices averaging around €10-€15 per person. Opening hours are typically from 8:00 AM to 10:00 PM.

Antiqvvm

For those seeking a fine dining experience, Antiqvvm provides an exquisite menu in a setting overlooking the Douro River. With a Michelin star to its name, the restaurant offers dishes that are both innovative and rooted in Portuguese tradition. Located at Rua de Entre-Quintas 220, the average price per person ranges from €70-€150, depending on the chosen menu and wine pairings. Reservations are recommended, and the restaurant operates from 12:30 PM to 3:00 PM and 7:30 PM to 11:00 PM.

Brasão Antas

Combining a cozy atmosphere with delectable dishes, Brasão Antas is known for its contemporary take on Portuguese cuisine. Favorites include the "Francesinha" and a variety of seafood options. Situated at Rua de Santa Justa 19, diners can expect to spend between €20-€30 per person. The restaurant welcomes guests from 12:00 PM to 11:00 PM.

Terra Nova

Located at Cais da Ribeira 34, Terra Nova offers a delightful dining experience with views of the Douro River. Specializing in seafood, particularly fresh oysters, the restaurant combines traditional flavors with modern presentation. Prices typically range from €25-€40 per person, and it operates from 12:00 PM to 11:00 PM.

Cantina 32

Nestled in the historic district, Cantina 32 is celebrated for its inventive approach to Portuguese cuisine. The rustic-chic decor adds to the ambiance, making it a popular choice among locals and tourists alike. Located at Rua das Flores 32, the average meal costs between €20-€35 per person. The restaurant is open from 12:00 PM to 3:00 PM and 7:00 PM to 11:00 PM.

Cafés

Porto boasts a vibrant café culture, blending historic charm with modern coffee trends. Here are some notable cafés to explore:

Café Majestic

Situated at Rua Santa Catarina 112, Café Majestic is a testament to Porto's rich history. Established in 1921, its Art Nouveau design, ornate interiors, and grand ambiance transport visitors to a bygone era. Beyond its architectural beauty, the café offers a selection of traditional Portuguese pastries and a variety of beverages. It's an ideal spot to savor a coffee while soaking in the historic atmosphere. Operating hours are from 9:30 AM to 11:30 PM daily.

Combi Coffee Roasters

Located at Rua do Morgado de Mateus 29, Combi Coffee Roasters is a haven for specialty coffee enthusiasts. They roast their beans in-house, ensuring fresh and flavorful brews. The minimalist décor and relaxed setting make it a favorite among locals and visitors alike. Prices are reasonable, with a cup of coffee averaging around €2.50. The café operates daily from 9:00 AM to 5:00 PM.

C'alma Coffee Room

Nestled at Rua de Passos Manuel 44, C'alma Coffee Room offers a serene environment away from the city's hustle. Housed in a traditional Portuguese building with high ceilings and vintage chandeliers, it provides a unique coffee experience. The café specializes in various brewing methods, including Chemex and Aeropress, catering to discerning coffee drinkers. Operating hours are Monday to Saturday, from 10:00 AM to 6:00 PM.

SO Coffee Roasters

Situated in the Cedofeita neighborhood, SO Coffee Roasters is committed to sustainable and fair-trade coffee practices. They offer a variety of brewing methods and a selection of pastries and light bites. The café's modern design and co-working space on the second floor make it a versatile spot for both relaxation and work. Prices are competitive, with espresso-based drinks starting at €2.00. Opening hours are from 9:00 AM to 6:00 PM daily.

Fábrica Coffee Roasters

With multiple locations in Porto, including Rua de José Falcão 122, Fábrica Coffee Roasters is known for its high-quality beans and cozy atmosphere. They provide a range of coffee options, from espresso to filter methods, ensuring something for every palate. The café also offers pastries and light snacks to complement their beverages. Operating hours vary by location but generally range from 8:00 AM to 7:00 PM.

Wine

Porto, renowned for its rich winemaking heritage, offers a variety of experiences for wine enthusiasts. Here's a guide to some notable wine cellars and tours in the city:

Sandeman Cellars

Located in Vila Nova de Gaia, Sandeman is one of the most iconic port wine producers. Visitors can explore the cellars, learn about the history of port wine, and enjoy tastings of their renowned selections. Tours are available daily from 10:00 AM to 6:00 PM, with prices starting at €15 per person. The address is Largo Miguel Bombarda 3, 4400-222 Vila Nova de Gaia.

Taylor's Port

Taylor's offers a comprehensive tour of its historic cellars, providing insights into the production and aging process of port wine. Guests can enjoy panoramic views of Porto from their terrace while sampling a range of ports. Tours operate daily from 10:00 AM to 7:00 PM, with prices starting at €15 per person. The address is Rua do Choupelo 250, 4400-088 Vila Nova de Gaia.

Graham's Lodge

Graham's Lodge combines tradition with modernity, offering guided tours that delve into the craftsmanship behind their port wines. The experience includes tastings paired with cheese or chocolate. Tours are available Monday to Friday from 9:30 AM to 6:00 PM, and weekends from 10:00 AM to 6:00 PM, with prices starting at €20 per person. The address is Rua do Agro 141, 4400-281 Vila Nova de Gaia.

Cálem Cellars

Cálem provides interactive tours that blend tradition with technology, including a 5D cinema experience showcasing the Douro region. The visit concludes with a tasting session accompanied by live Fado music. Tours run daily from 10:00 AM to 7:00 PM, with prices starting at €15 per person. The address is Avenida de Diogo Leite 344, 4400-111 Vila Nova de Gaia.

Ferreira Cellars

Ferreira is a historic name in port wine, with roots dating back to 1751. Their cellars offer a journey through time, highlighting the legacy of Dona Antónia Adelaide Ferreira. Tours are available daily from 10:00 AM to 6:00 PM, with prices starting at €12 per person. The address is Avenida Ramos Pinto 70, 4400-266 Vila Nova de Gaia.

Markets

Porto's vibrant markets offer a glimpse into the city's rich culture and daily life. Here are some noteworthy markets to explore:

Mercado do Bolhão

Established in 1837, Mercado do Bolhão is a historic open-air market located at Rua Formosa 322. After a four-year renovation, it reopened in 2022, retaining its traditional charm. The market houses around 80 stalls over three floors, offering fresh produce, fish, meat, and local wines, alongside newer coffee shops and restaurants. It's open Monday to Friday from 8:00 AM to 8:00 PM, and Saturdays from 8:00 AM to 6:00 PM.

Porto Belo Market

Inspired by London's Portobello Road Market, Porto Belo Market is held every Saturday at Praça de Carlos Alberto from 10:00 AM to 7:00 PM. Vendors offer vintage clothing, vinyl records, handmade crafts, and organic products, making it a treasure trove for unique finds.

Mercado Municipal de Matosinhos

Located near the port in Matosinhos, this market is renowned for its fresh seafood. Fishermen deliver their catch daily, providing a wide selection of fish and shellfish. Nearby, Rua Heróis de França offers numerous seafood restaurants where visitors can savor the day's catch.

Mercado Bom Sucesso

Housed in a historic building, Mercado Bom Sucesso has transformed into a modern food court featuring various food stalls, cafes, and shops. It's an excellent spot to sample local delicacies like pastéis de nata and francesinha. The market operates daily from 8:00 AM to 11:00 PM, extending to midnight on Saturdays.

Feira da Vandoma

Feira da Vandoma is a traditional flea market held every Saturday from 8:00 AM to 1:00 PM at Rua de Diu 365. Vendors sell second-hand items such as clothes, books, furniture, and antiques, attracting both locals and tourists seeking unique bargains.

Where to Stay

Hotels

Porto offers a diverse range of accommodations, from luxurious palaces to contemporary boutique hotels, catering to various preferences and budgets. Here are some notable options:

The Yeatman

Perched in Vila Nova de Gaia, The Yeatman is a luxury wine hotel offering panoramic views of Porto and the Douro River. Each room is designed with wine-themed décor, and the hotel boasts a Michelin-starred restaurant. Amenities include an extensive wine cellar, a Caudalie Vinothérapie® Spa, and indoor and outdoor pools. Room rates start at approximately €250 per night. The address is Rua do Choupelo 88, 4400-088 Vila Nova de Gaia.

Torel 1884

Situated in the heart of Porto, Torel 1884 is a boutique hotel inspired by the Age of Discovery. Each room and suite is uniquely decorated, reflecting themes from Africa, Asia, and South America. Guests can enjoy the on-site Bartolomeu Bistro & Wine bar. Room rates begin at around €150 per night. The hotel is located at Rua de Mouzinho da Silveira 228, 4050-417 Porto.

PortoBay Flores

Set within a 16th-century palace, PortoBay Flores seamlessly blends historic charm with modern luxury. The hotel features 66 rooms, a spa, an indoor pool, and the acclaimed restaurant, Bistrô Flores. Its central location provides easy access to major attractions. Rates start at approximately €200 per night. The address is Rua das Flores 27, 4050-416 Porto.

Maison Albar Hotels Le Monumental Palace

This five-star hotel combines French elegance with Portuguese hospitality. Located in a restored historic building, it offers 76 rooms and suites, multiple dining venues, a spa, and an indoor pool. Room rates start at around €300 per night. The hotel is situated at Avenida dos Aliados 151, 4000-067 Porto.

Rosa Et Al Townhouse

Located in the artsy neighborhood of Cedofeita, this boutique guesthouse offers a cozy atmosphere with just six suites. Guests can enjoy a garden, a concept store, and an on-site restaurant serving brunch and afternoon tea. Rates begin at approximately €130 per night. The address is Rua do Rosário 233, 4050-524 Porto.

Hostels

Porto offers a variety of hostels catering to diverse traveler preferences. Here are some notable options:

Rivoli Cinema Hostel

Located in the heart of Porto, Rivoli Cinema Hostel offers a unique cinematic theme throughout its premises. Guests can enjoy a rooftop terrace, communal kitchen, and a cozy lounge area. Dormitory beds start at approximately €20 per night, while private rooms are available at higher rates. The hostel is situated at Rua Dr. Magalhães Lemos 83, 4000-332 Porto.

The Passenger Hostel

Nestled within São Bento Train Station, The Passenger Hostel provides a unique lodging experience. Guests can choose from dormitory beds starting around €25 per night or private rooms at higher rates. The address is Estação de São Bento, Praça de Almeida Garrett, 4000-069 Porto.

Gallery Hostel

Combining art and hospitality, Gallery Hostel is located in the artsy Miguel Bombarda district. The hostel features art exhibitions, a bar, and a garden. Dormitory beds start at *approximately €22 per night, with private rooms also available. Find it at Rua de Miguel Bombarda 222, 4050-377 Porto.*

Selina Porto

Situated in Porto's vibrant Cedofeita neighborhood, Selina Porto offers a lively atmosphere with regular events, a co-working space, and a garden. Dormitory beds start at around €18 per night, and private accommodations are also available. The hostel is located at Rua das Oliveiras 61, 4050-449 Porto.

Porto Lounge Hostel & Guesthouse

Porto Lounge Hostel & Guesthouse offers a blend of modern design and classic architecture. Amenities include a shared kitchen, lounge areas, and organized events. Dormitory beds start at approximately €19 per night, with private rooms also available. The address is Rua do Almada 317, 4050-038 Porto.

Boutique

Porto boasts a selection of boutique hotels that blend historic charm with modern luxury, offering personalized experiences for discerning travelers. Here are some notable options:

Torel 1884 Suites & Apartments

Situated in the heart of Porto, Torel 1884 draws inspiration from Portugal's Age of Discovery, with each floor themed around continents explored by Portuguese navigators. The hotel offers 12 suites and 11 apartments, each uniquely designed to reflect the spirit of exploration. Guests can enjoy the on-site Bartolomeu Bistro & Wine bar, serving a curated selection of local wines and tapas. Room rates start at approximately €150 per night. The address is Rua de Mouzinho da Silveira 228, 4050-417 Porto.

Rosa Et Al Townhouse

Nestled in Porto's arts district, Rosa Et Al Townhouse offers a cozy atmosphere with six individually decorated suites. The townhouse emphasizes slow living, providing in-room spa treatments and a garden where guests can relax. The on-site restaurant serves brunch and afternoon tea, focusing on organic and locally sourced ingredients. Room rates begin at around €130 per night. The address is Rua do Rosário 233, 4050-524 Porto.

Vinha Boutique Hotel

Located on the banks of the Douro River, Vinha Boutique Hotel combines luxury with tranquility. The property features lush gardens, a spa, and an outdoor pool, providing a serene retreat from the bustling city. Each room is elegantly designed, blending classic and contemporary elements. Room rates start at approximately €200 per night. The address is Rua de São João da Foz 1, 4150-413 Porto.

Descobertas Boutique Hotel by Aspasios

Situated in Porto's historic Ribeira district, Descobertas Boutique Hotel offers modern accommodations inspired by the Portuguese Discoveries. Each floor reflects a different destination explored by Portuguese navigators, providing a unique cultural experience. The hotel provides free Wi-Fi throughout the building and is within walking distance of major attractions. Room rates start at around €100 per night. The address is Rua Fonte Taurina 14-22, 4050-269 Porto.

Airbnb

Porto offers a diverse range of Airbnb accommodations to suit various preferences and budgets. Here are some notable options:

Magic Escape Apartments 1 - Douro River Views

Located in Vila Nova de Gaia, this fully renovated apartment provides stunning views of Porto's landmarks. It's within walking distance to port wine cellars and downtown Porto. The spacious apartment accommodates up to six guests, offering free Wi-Fi and parking. Rates start at approximately €120 per night.

LUXURY PENTHOUSE - River Gallery Art - View & Center

Situated directly across the Douro River, this luxury penthouse boasts views of the Luis I Bridge. Guests have easy access to boat rides, the World of Wine (WOW) cultural district, and the historic center. The apartment features modern amenities and stylish decor. Rates begin at around €150 per night.

Say Cheese Apt (Downtown) with Heating

This cozy apartment, renovated in 2017, blends 1950s architecture with modern comforts. Located in the traditional downtown area of Carlos Alberto, it offers air conditioning and minimalist decor. Ideal for couples or solo travelers, rates start at approximately €80 per night.

For a comprehensive selection of Airbnb accommodations in Porto, you can visit their official website.

Nightlife

Bars

Porto's vibrant nightlife offers a diverse array of bars, each providing unique experiences that cater to various tastes. Here are some notable establishments to consider:

Capela Incomum

Housed within a 19th-century chapel, Capela Incomum offers a distinctive ambiance where guests can enjoy a curated selection of wines and cocktails. The intimate setting, characterized by its antique decor, provides a serene atmosphere ideal for relaxed conversations. Located at Travessa do Carregal 77, 4050-167 Porto, this bar typically operates from 6:00 PM to midnight.

Base Porto

Situated in an open garden space, Base Porto is an outdoor bar that hosts local DJs, creating a lively atmosphere. Guests can enjoy a Super Bock beer or a cocktail while mingling in a relaxed setting. Operating hours may vary, so it's advisable to check their schedule before visiting.

Aduela

Aduela is a beloved spot among locals for after-work refreshments, offering Portuguese wines from several regions at affordable prices, as well as sangria and moscatel. The bar also serves classic Portuguese sandwiches, tremoços, and grissini. If the terrace is full, patrons often take their drinks and sit on the street, embracing the communal vibe. Located at Rua das Oliveiras 36, 4050-449 Porto, Aduela typically operates from early afternoon until late at night.

17° Panoramic Bar

Perched on the 17th floor of the Hotel Dom Henrique, this bar offers a 360-degree view of Porto. Guests can enjoy a variety of drinks while taking in the city's skyline. The bar operates daily from 12:00 PM to 2:00 AM. It's located at Rua do Bolhão 223, 4000-112 Porto.

Portugal, Porto

Fado

Porto offers a variety of venues where visitors can experience the soulful melodies of Fado, Portugal's traditional music genre. Here are some notable establishments:

Ideal Clube de Fado

Ideal Clube de Fado is renowned for its authentic performances, emphasizing traditional Fado without modern fusion. Guests are introduced to the history and nuances of Fado, enhancing their appreciation of the art form. The club hosts three concerts daily at 6:00 PM, 7:30 PM, and 9:00 PM. Tickets are priced at €19 for adults, €14 for youths aged 6 to 17, and free for children under 6. Each ticket includes a glass of Port wine or water. The venue is located at Rua do Ateneu Comercial do Porto 32, 4000-380 Porto.

O Fado Maior do Porto

O Fado Maior do Porto offers a unique experience by showcasing both traditional Fado and Coimbra Fado, the latter being a style associated with university students from Coimbra. The intimate setting allows for a close connection with the performers. Shows are held daily at 7:00 PM. Tickets are priced at €14 and include a glass of Port wine or water.

The venue is situated at Rua de São João Novo 16, 4050-293 Porto.

Calém Port Wine Cellars

For those interested in combining Fado with wine tasting, Calém Port Wine Cellars offers a compelling option. Visitors can tour the cellars, sample Port wines, and enjoy a live Fado performance amidst the aging barrels. This combined experience provides insight into two integral aspects of Portuguese culture. Tickets are available for €25, which includes the tour, tasting, and show. The cellars are located at Avenida de Diogo Leite 344, 4400-111 Vila Nova de Gaia.

Casa da Guitarra

Casa da Guitarra is both a musical instrument store and a venue for intimate Fado concerts. The setting provides excellent acoustics, enhancing the overall experience. Shows are held daily at 6:00 PM and 7:30 PM. Tickets are priced at €18 for adults, €16 for youths aged 13 to 18, and €15 for children aged 3 to 12, each including a glass of Port wine. The address is Avenida Vimara Peres 49, 4000-545 Porto.

Fado na Baixa

Located in the heart of Porto, Fado na Baixa offers curated shows that delve into the history and soul of Fado. The venue aims to provide an immersive experience, bringing audiences closer to the essence of this musical tradition. Performances are held daily at 6:00 PM and 7:30 PM. Tickets cost €19 for adults, €16 for youths aged 13 to 18, and €12 for children aged 3 to 12. Each ticket includes a glass of Port wine. The venue is located at Rua de São João 99, 4050-553 Porto.

Portugal, Porto, River

Rooftops

Porto offers a variety of rooftop bars that provide stunning views of the city and the Douro River. Here are some notable options:

Douro Sky Lounge

Located atop the Vincci Porto Hotel, the Douro Sky Lounge offers panoramic views of the Douro River, with the Ponte da Arrábida in the background. The lounge features an eclectic mix of bar stools and sofa lounges, suitable for both lively gatherings and intimate conversations. Guests can enjoy a variety of tapas, burgers, and carefully crafted cocktails. The lounge operates daily from 1:00 PM to 11:30 PM and is situated at Rua Alameda Basilio Teles 29-33, 4150-127 Porto.

LIFT Rooftop Via Catarina

Perched on the 14th floor of the Via Catarina Shopping Centre, LIFT Rooftop Via Catarina provides expansive views of Porto. The ambiance resembles a garden setting, offering a relaxed atmosphere. The menu includes açaí bowls, cheese boards, seasonal salads, and creative cocktails. Operating hours are Monday to Thursday from noon to 11:00 PM, Friday and Saturday from noon to midnight, and Sunday from noon to 10:00 PM. The address is Rua Santa Catarina 312-350, 14th Floor, 4000-443 Porto.

17º Restaurante & Bar

Situated on the 17th floor of Hotel Dom Henrique, 17º Restaurante & Bar offers panoramic views of Porto's historic center and the Douro River. The contemporary decor and stylish furnishings create an elegant atmosphere. Guests can indulge in exquisite cuisine, including fresh seafood dishes, tender meats, and vegetarian options, complemented by a selection of wines and cocktails. Located at Rua do Bolhão 223, 4000-112 Porto, the bar operates daily from 12:00 PM to 2:00 AM.

Terrace Lounge 360º

Perched atop Espaço Porto Cruz in Vila Nova de Gaia, Terrace Lounge 360º offers a 360-degree view of Porto and the Douro River. The bar provides a selection of wines, cocktails, and light snacks. It's an ideal spot to enjoy the sunset over the city. The address is Largo Miguel Bombarda 23, 4400-222 Vila Nova de Gaia.

Music

Porto's music scene is vibrant and diverse, offering a variety of venues that cater to different musical tastes. Here are some notable spots to experience live music in the city:

Casa da Música

Located at Avenida da Boavista 604-610, 4149-071 Porto, Casa da Música is an iconic concert hall designed by architect Rem Koolhaas. Since its opening in 2005, it has become a central hub for music lovers, hosting a wide range of performances from classical symphonies to contemporary bands. The building's unique architecture and acoustics make it a must-visit venue. Ticket prices and showtimes vary depending on the event, so it's advisable to check their official website for the latest information.

Hot Five Jazz & Blues Club

Situated at Rua de Guerra Junqueiro 495, 4000-294 Porto, Hot Five Jazz & Blues Club offers an intimate setting for jazz and blues enthusiasts. The club features live performances from both local and international artists, creating a cozy atmosphere reminiscent of classic jazz bars. It's a perfect spot to enjoy soulful music accompanied by a selection of drinks. Operating hours typically start in the evening, with performances commencing around 10:00 PM. Entrance fees vary depending on the night's lineup.

Maus Hábitos

Located at Rua de Passos Manuel 178, 4th Floor, 4000-382 Porto, Maus Hábitos is a cultural space that blends art, music, and gastronomy. The venue hosts live music events spanning various genres, from indie rock to electronic beats. Its eclectic programming ensures there's always something new to experience. In addition to concerts, Maus Hábitos also features art exhibitions and a restaurant, making it a multifaceted cultural hub. Operating hours and event schedules vary, so it's best to consult their official channels for the latest updates.

Hard Club

Situated in the historic Mercado Ferreira Borges at Praça do Infante Dom Henrique, 4050-252 Porto, Hard Club is a versatile venue that hosts concerts, exhibitions, and cultural events. The space is known for its diverse lineup, featuring both local talent and international acts across genres like rock, metal, and electronic music. The venue also houses a restaurant and bar, providing a complete entertainment experience. Event schedules and ticket prices vary, so checking their official website is recommended for the most current information.

Education

Schools

Porto boasts a diverse educational landscape, encompassing esteemed international schools and universities that cater to both local and international communities.

International Schools in Porto

Oporto British School

Established in 1894, Oporto British School is among the oldest British schools in mainland Europe. It offers a curriculum based on the British educational system, serving students aged 3 to 18. The school emphasizes holistic development, integrating academics with extracurricular activities. Tuition fees range from €7,988 to €14,585 annually, depending on the student's grade level. The campus is located at Rua da Cerca, 326/350, 4150-201 Porto.

CLIP – The Oporto International School

Founded in 1988, CLIP offers an international curriculum tailored to foster academic excellence and personal growth. The school caters to students from pre-kindergarten to year

12, with instruction primarily in English. Annual tuition fees range from €7,585 to €10,945, varying by grade level. The school is situated at Rua de Vila Nova, 1071, 4100-506 Porto.

Lycée Français International de Porto

This institution provides a French-based curriculum, welcoming students from kindergarten through high school. It emphasizes multilingual education, offering instruction in French, Portuguese, and English. Tuition fees vary based on the student's grade and specific program. The school is located at Rua Gil Eanes, 533, 4150-348 Porto.

Deutsche Schule zu Porto

Catering to the German-speaking community and others interested in a German curriculum, this school serves students from kindergarten to 12th grade. It focuses on fostering cultural ties between Portugal and Germany. Tuition fees depend on the student's grade level and specific requirements. The school is situated at Rua Guerra Junqueiro, 162, 4150-386 Porto.

CJD International School

Established in 1934, CJD International School is one of Porto's oldest educational institutions. It offers a curriculum that blends international education standards with local *cultural elements, serving students from primary through secondary levels. Tuition fees and specific programs can be obtained directly from the school's administration. The school is located at Rua de Santa Isabel, 151, 4250-536 Porto.*

Universities in Porto

University of Porto

Founded in 1911, the University of Porto is one of Portugal's largest and most prestigious public universities. It offers a wide array of undergraduate, master's, and doctoral programs across various fields. The university is recognized for its research output and ranks among the top institutions in Europe. Tuition fees for international students vary depending on the program and level of study. The main campus is located at Praça de Gomes Teixeira, 4099-002 Porto.

Polytechnic Institute of Porto

Established in 1985, this public institution offers diverse programs in engineering, management, education, and health technologies. It focuses on applied research and practical training, preparing students for the professional world. Tuition fees and program details can be found on the institute's official website. The main campus is at Rua Dr. Roberto Frias, 602, 4200-465 Porto.

Fernando Pessoa University

A private university founded in 1996, Fernando Pessoa University offers programs in health sciences, human and social sciences, and science and technology. It emphasizes research and community engagement. Tuition fees vary by program and student nationality. The university is located at Praça 9 de Abril, 349, 4249-004 Porto.

Lusophone University of Porto

Part of the Lusophone Group, this university offers programs in communication, arts, economics, and engineering. It aims to promote Lusophone culture and language. Tuition fees and program specifics are available on the university's website. The campus is situated at Rua Augusto Rosa, 24, 4000-098 Porto.

Nursing School of Porto

Specializing in nursing education, this public institution offers undergraduate and postgraduate programs focused on healthcare. It collaborates with various hospitals and health centers for practical training. Tuition fees depend on the program and student status. The school is located at Rua Dr. António Bernardino de Almeida, 400, 4200-072 Porto.

Porto's educational institutions provide a wide range of options for families and students seeking quality education, from early childhood through advanced university degrees.

Universities

Porto is home to several esteemed universities that cater to a diverse student population. Here are some notable institutions:

University of Porto

Established in 1911, the University of Porto (Universidade do Porto) is a prominent public research university. It is the second-largest university in Portugal by enrollment and is recognized for its significant research contributions. The university comprises multiple faculties, including sciences, arts, engineering, and medicine. It consistently ranks among the top Portuguese universities and holds a reputable position in international rankings.

Polytechnic Institute of Porto

Founded in 1985, the Polytechnic Institute of Porto (Instituto Politécnico do Porto) is a public institution offering a range of undergraduate and postgraduate programs. It focuses on applied sciences and technologies, providing students with practical and industry-relevant education.

Fernando Pessoa University

Established in 1996, Fernando Pessoa University (Universidade Fernando Pessoa) is a private institution named after the renowned Portuguese poet. It offers various programs across disciplines such as health sciences, social sciences, and humanities. The university emphasizes research and community engagement.

Lusophone University of Porto

The Lusophone University of Porto (Universidade Lusófona do Porto) is part of the larger Lusophone group of institutions. It offers programs in fields like communication, arts, economics, and engineering. The university aims to promote Lusophone culture and language.

Tips

Porto on a beautiful summer day. Porto, Portugal.

Safety

Porto is generally considered a safe city for travelers, with low crime rates compared to other major European destinations. However, like any urban area, it's essential to remain vigilant and take standard precautions to ensure a trouble-free visit.

Petty crimes, such as pickpocketing and bag snatching, are the most common concerns, particularly in crowded tourist spots, public transportation, and busy streets. To minimize risks, keep personal belongings secure, avoid displaying valuables, and stay attentive to your surroundings.

While violent crime is rare, incidents can occur, especially in nightlife areas or during late hours. It's advisable to avoid poorly lit or deserted streets after dark and opt for reputable transportation options when returning to accommodations.

Etiquette

Porto, Portugal's second-largest city, boasts a rich cultural heritage that is deeply rooted in traditional customs and social norms. Understanding and respecting local etiquette can enhance your experience and foster positive interactions with residents.

Greetings

In Porto, greetings are often formal yet warm. Men typically shake hands with direct eye contact, while women may exchange two kisses on the cheek, starting with the right. In professional settings, a firm handshake is standard. It's customary to use titles such as 'Senhor' (Mr.) or 'Senhora' (Mrs.) followed by the person's surname until invited to use their first name.

Punctuality

Punctuality varies depending on the context. For social gatherings, arriving 10 to 15 minutes late is acceptable and often expected. However, in business settings, punctuality is valued, and arriving on time demonstrates professionalism and respect.

Dress Code

Porto residents tend to dress conservatively and elegantly. While casual attire is acceptable, it's advisable to opt for neat and well-coordinated outfits. Overly revealing clothing is generally discouraged, especially in religious or formal settings.

Dining Etiquette

When dining in Porto, wait to be seated by the host and keep your hands visible on the table, avoiding placing elbows on it. Begin eating only after the host says "bom apetite." Using utensils for most foods is customary, and leaving a small amount of food on your plate indicates satisfaction.

Gift Giving

If invited to a Portuguese home, bringing a small gift such as flowers, quality chocolates, or a good bottle of wine is appreciated. Avoid giving lilies or chrysanthemums, as they are associated with funerals, and refrain from gifting anything in quantities of 13, as this number is considered unlucky.

Communication Style

The Portuguese communication style is generally reserved and formal. They value politeness and may not be as direct as some cultures. It's important to listen attentively and avoid interrupting others during conversations. Using excessive hand gestures or being overly demonstrative is uncommon and may be viewed as inappropriate.

Money

Porto, Portugal's second-largest city, uses the euro (€) as its official currency. The euro is divided into 100 cents, with coins available in denominations of 1, 2, 5, 10, 20, and 50 cents, as well as €1 and €2. Banknotes come in €5, €10, €20, €50, €100, €200, and €500 denominations.

Currency Exchange

Travelers can exchange foreign currencies at banks, exchange bureaus, and some hotels in Porto. It's advisable to compare rates and fees before exchanging money to ensure you receive a fair deal. Additionally, many visitors find it convenient to withdraw euros directly from ATMs using their home bank cards, often securing favorable exchange rates.

ATMs and Banking Services

ATMs, locally known as "Multibanco," are widely available throughout Porto, offering services beyond cash withdrawals, such as purchasing tickets and making transfers. These machines typically accept international cards, including Visa and Mastercard. However, it's prudent to inform your bank of your travel plans to prevent any security blocks on your card.

Credit and Debit Card Usage

Credit and debit cards are commonly accepted in Porto, especially in hotels, restaurants, and larger retail stores. Visa and Mastercard are the most widely recognized, while American Express may not be accepted everywhere. Despite the widespread card acceptance, carrying some cash is advisable for small businesses, markets, or in situations where card payments might not be possible.

Tipping Etiquette

Tipping in Porto is appreciated but not obligatory. In restaurants, rounding up the bill or leaving a tip of 5-10% for good service is customary. For taxi drivers, rounding up the fare is common practice. Porters and hotel staff may also appreciate a small gratuity for their services.

Tax Refunds

Non-European Union residents are eligible for tax refunds on purchases made in Portugal. To qualify, shop at stores displaying the "Tax-Free Shopping" logo and request a tax-free form upon purchase. Present this form, along with your purchases and passport, at the customs desk upon departure to process your refund.

By familiarizing yourself with Porto's monetary practices, you can navigate financial transactions confidently and enjoy a seamless experience in this vibrant city.

Phrases

Learning some basic Portuguese phrases can greatly enhance your experience when visiting Porto. Here are some essential expressions to help you navigate daily interactions:

Greetings and Common Expressions

Hello: "Olá"

Good morning: "Bom dia"

Good afternoon: "Boa tarde"

Good evening/night: "Boa noite"

How are you?: "Como está?"

I'm fine: "Estou bem"

Please: "Por favor"

Thank you: "Obrigado" (if you're male) / "Obrigada" (if you're female)

Yes: "Sim"

No: "Não"

Excuse me/Sorry: "Desculpe"

Useful Questions

Do you speak English?: "Você fala inglês?"

I don't understand: "Eu não entendo"

Where is the bathroom?: "Onde fica o banheiro?"

How much does this cost?: "Quanto custa isso?"

Where is...?: "Onde está...?"

Dining and Shopping

I would like...: "Eu gostaria..."

Check, please: "A conta, por favor"

Delicious: "Delicioso"

Water: "Água"

Wine: "Vinho"

Beer: "Cerveja"

view of the old city center of Porto

Conclusion

Porto is a city that captivates visitors with its blend of history, culture, gastronomy, and scenic beauty. Whether you are wandering through the cobbled streets of Ribeira, admiring the iconic Dom Luís I Bridge, or savoring a glass of world-famous Port wine in Vila Nova de Gaia, the city offers a rich and immersive experience. With its welcoming atmosphere, diverse neighborhoods, and an ever-growing cultural scene, Porto continues to be one of Europe's most cherished destinations.

Throughout this guide, we have explored the best that Porto has to offer, from its historic sites and vibrant markets to its culinary delights and thriving nightlife. The city's deep-rooted traditions, seen in its festivals, Fado music, and local craftsmanship, provide an authentic Portuguese experience. Meanwhile, its modern attractions, including rooftop bars, contemporary art galleries, and innovative gastronomy, showcase a city that is constantly evolving while preserving its heritage.

Getting around Porto is easy, with a well-connected public transportation system and plenty of pedestrian-friendly areas. The city's compact size allows visitors to explore its many districts at a leisurely pace, taking in breathtaking views *along the Douro River and discovering hidden gems in its lesser-known streets. Whether you prefer an active itinerary filled with sightseeing and adventure or a more relaxed trip enjoying the cafés, parks, and river cruises, Porto caters to every type of traveler.*

Accommodations range from luxurious boutique hotels to budget-friendly hostels and unique Airbnb stays, ensuring that visitors can find a comfortable place to rest, regardless of their budget. Dining in Porto is a highlight of any trip, with a mix of traditional dishes, fresh seafood, and contemporary cuisine that reflects the city's dynamic food scene. From a simple pastel de nata and espresso at a local café to a multi-course meal at a Michelin-starred restaurant, every bite in Porto tells a story.

For those seeking a deeper understanding of the city, engaging with the locals is key. The people of Porto are known for their friendliness and hospitality, and a few simple Portuguese phrases can go a long way in enhancing interactions. Respecting local customs and etiquette, whether at a family-run restaurant or a Fado performance, enriches the travel experience and fosters meaningful connections.

Porto's charm extends beyond the city itself. The surrounding region offers incredible day trips, from the terraced vineyards of the Douro Valley to the golden beaches of the Atlantic coast. Whether visiting medieval towns, exploring nature trails, or sampling some of the finest wines in the world, the broader Porto area provides endless opportunities for adventure and discovery.

This guide has aimed to provide a comprehensive resource for navigating Porto and making the most of your time in this enchanting city. Whether it is your first visit or a return trip, Porto's timeless appeal ensures there is always something new to experience. From its architectural wonders and artistic treasures to its lively bars and tranquil gardens, the city leaves a lasting impression on all who visit.

As you explore Porto, take the time to slow down and absorb the essence of the city—the rhythm of daily life, the aroma of fresh pastries in the morning, the sight of laundry hanging from balconies, the sound of waves crashing along Foz do Douro, and the warmth of a local greeting you with a smile. These are the moments that make Porto truly special.

With its balance of tradition and innovation, history and modernity, Porto is more than just a travel destination—it is a city that invites you to return, time and time again.

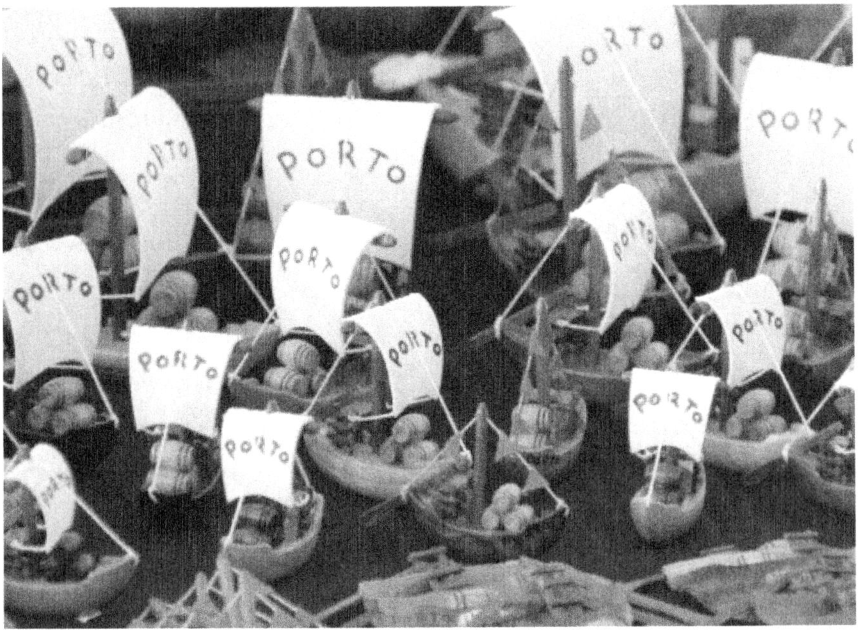
PORTO

Printed in Dunstable, United Kingdom